CALL OF TH[E]

Volume I

"NOT ALL GARGOYLES ARE THERE
TO PROTECT YOU"

By

Robbie S Stephens

Copyright 2023 by Robbie S Stephens.

All rights reserved. No part of this publication may be reproduced, stored, or transmitted in any form or by any means, either electronic, mechanical, photocopying, recording, scanning or otherwise, without the expressed written permission from the Author. It is illegal to copy this book, post it to a website, or distribute it by other means without permission, except for the use of brief quotations in a book review.

Robbie S Stephens asserts the moral right to be identified as the author of this book.

Table of Contents

Dedication ii

Acknowledgement iii

About the Author v

Chapter One CPC464 3

Chapter Two Tea with Two.. 33

Chapter Three The Royal Connection............................ 51

Chapter Four And They're Off.. 61

Chapter Five Something's Wrong 71

Chapter Six Do you Know why you're here?................. 87

Chapter Seven The Gargoyle Returns............................ 99

Chapter Eight The Brick Walls...................................... 105

Chapter Nine The Diary Entry...................................... 119

Chapter Ten The High Commissioners Son................. 135

Chapter Eleven Overthinking 151

Chapter Twelve The Otters 165

Chapter Thirteen My Thoughts 179

Chapter Fourteen Jesus, he Knows Me 187

Chapter Fifteen The Quotes.. 201

This is a true story

It's my story

Dedication

986166

2071

2023

Acknowledgement

There are a few people that I would like to thank for helping me with my story.

Thank you to Noah and Mr Roberts for being decent human beings and for all the fishing tips.

Thank you to my Mum and Dad for everything you have ever done for me. Not only now but my entire life, you have both always been there, and I love you both so very much.

The rest of my family thank you for having my back and encouraging me, even though sometimes I ignore it. Thank you for giving me a reason to be happy and holding my hand.

Thank you to Rachel Bedwell from

First Light and Ground 2 Grow Therapy Swindon

www.ground2growtherapy.com

Thank you to Cerian Lye-Owens

www.heartspace.me.uk

and all the team at IPSUM Swindon

www.ipsum.care

But most of all, thank you to my wife

You have been truly amazing, and I can't tell you how much I love you. You have made me a very happy man, and I can't wait to spend the rest of our lives together.

You are my rock. I love you to the Death Star and Back.

About the Author

I always laughed and joked when I was younger, that I would be dead by the time I'm 40 and I would write a book all about my life. Well, I'm now 47, I think. Maybe 48, if I'm honest I couldn't tell you what year we are living in right now.

You're reading this so I guess half of it came true.

I've had a crazy life.

What would you do if you were abused as a child and then shared with his friends their little play thing?

Would you want to talk about it?

It was all my fault, wasn't it? I let it happen?

This is my story

I've been hiding it for over 30 years.

The shame and the guilt that I still hold onto to this day.

My intention was to

"Take it to the grave"

You once said to me

"No one will believe you"

You were my friend, and I trusted you.

I believed what you said was true.

30 years later, I realise that it was all a lie.

What you did was wrong,

You groomed me, and then you abused me.

You weren't my friend at all!

Everything you are about to read is real

It's not make belief. I desperately wish it was.

This is the story of my life, the ups and the downs, the brutal truth about Mental Health.

I would like to take this opportunity to say sorry for the way this book is presented. All the words are flowing out of my head as I'm typing them and as I'm hearing them.

Sorry if my story is a little disjointed, and I keep repeating myself. I didn't want the publishers to mess around with it too much, making all the sentences and paragraphs neat and tidy. That's not how my head works.

I have severe Mental Health issues at the moment, and It's my story. I have to write about how it happened.

Bear with it, though; it's a crazy one, and some days, even I don't believe it can be real.

Also, I have made reference to quite a lot of brand names, so I just wanted to say.

"Other brands are available"

Although some of the wording may be slightly different from what was actually said at the time, but in all fairness, it was a long time ago.

This is how I remember it.

Exactly how I remember it!

My ultimate aim in writing this book is for me. It's for me to finally speak out and tell the world what happened to me all those years ago. I have no idea why my brain is feeling this way at the moment. It just does.

I've wanted to shout it from the rooftops, but I simply didn't think I would ever be believed.

Why would you? He was an adult, and I was a child!

At the moment, I want to change the world and to speak out about Mental Health and how it really is. What it's like living with this thing inside your body, inside your head.

If you're reading this, then I have made the decision to get it published in the hope that somewhere out there, someone will finally have the courage to do what I have just done.

To speak out about what happened or is currently happening to you, to finally have the strength and belief that you are not alone and you will be believed. That help is out there, and people are kind; people love you.

I'm sorry if when you read this book, it triggers you off, bringing up old wounds, flashbacks and more, even opening new wounds that so desperately need healing.

I want millions of people to read this and to come forward to receive the help they need, the help that you might need. The help that you so desperately deserve.

To try to understand and make sense of it all.

So far, this book has saved one person. That person is me.

So, it was all worth it.

For me, I find it both hard and easy to read this. After all, I wrote it. I know what the voices inside my head are telling me; I can see the images that I describe, and I know the tone of my voice when I'm talking.

It's my first time writing a proper book like this, so I have no idea how to construct it, where paragraphs need to be, or where full stops and commas need to go.

So, I googled how many commas can you put in a book. About one or two per sentence is fine, just in case you were wondering.

I don't even know what a comma does!

I didn't do that great at school. However, I still managed a Grade C in English Literature and English Language. To me, a comma represents a pause in a sentence, just a brief moment to catch my breath or maybe sit and think for a second. Simply a slight change in the tone of my voice or how I have sped up or slowed down.

Reading this makes total sense to me, and I hope it does to you, too. I hope you can hear my voice as we go along this journey together.

The Pain and the Suffering, the guilt and shame that I still feel to this day.

I will guide you through my head and try to explain how it feels living with a Mental Health Condition.

Try and read this as I intend, give a little pause on the commas and immerse yourself in the world that I currently call home, this strange world I live in.

Really try hard to put the words I'm telling you into the story. Try to picture the Gargoyles. It's not that hard. There's one on the front cover. Only mine was plastic and painted red.

See if you can pick up on the many hints and tips that I'm trying to give you along the way. See if you can spot the many '80s references I've tried to sneak in.

I loved the 80's. It was the best time ever.

"Get Ready"

That was the start of an 80's classic Video game called

"Out Run".

I loved playing Video Games, and that was one of my favourites.

Where it all started, Kowloon Hong Kong 1976.

Chapter One
CPC464

Amstrad CPC464, I loved that computer. It was probably the best thing I owned. I would spend hours and hours typing code for some Star Wars game, only to get it all wrong and have to go back through it all again. Line by line, one finger typing at a time, I would sit in my bedroom for hours playing video games. It shouldn't be funny, but I bet most of us have done it. After all, it was the late 80s or early 90s. I must have been about 14 years old. I would visit my local corner shop; you could buy video games on cassette. I could never afford the good ones, just the old stuff, really. You would go in and buy a game, then race home as fast as your legs could cycle. In what I would consider the olden days, you could record the sound from one cassette tape to another. With the little help of another blank cassette and a little bit of sticky tape in the corners, that always did the trick.

Most kids my age must have had a small boom box type thing. A cassette stereo system. Any younger people reading this, you may want to google what a tape cassette is and some other bits in this book, to be fair. You would make a pirate copy of the video games, but the best part was you could take the game back to the shop later that day and say you didn't want it anymore, then get a refund. I was even asked the question once by the storekeeper.

"Are you making pirate copies of these at home?"

I was, but damned if I was going to admit it. I didn't want to spend my £2 pocket money on games, not when I could get them for free.

I worked for that little corner shop as a paperboy for a while, in the early mornings, no matter what the weather was. Sundays, I would go in early and number the papers up for the rest of the lads, just me and the storekeeper.

Sunday's bags were always bulging!

I started as a paperboy in the winter, just two weeks before Christmas. The other lad had quit for some reason. It was amazing all the tips I was given, all them Christmas bonuses the people would give me for a year's worth of hard work. The reality was it was only two weeks, I had loads of money, maybe £6 a week, and it all went on sweets and stickers.

We had a little shop in the town that sold penny sweets, half penny sweets, in fact. You would go in and grab a small white paper bag, fill it with the sweets you wanted, and then go and pay. One hundred penny sweets were a lot back then. The bag always had one hundred and ten in it, though.

"Sorry, miscounted!"

The shopkeeper very rarely checked or counted them out, though. You would try and time it for when someone else was in the shop, another customer just about to pay. You certainly didn't want to be the last lad amongst your mates, the one who always got checked. The last man always had to stick to the rules no matter what! The rest of my money would go on football cards, the Panini Albums. Constantly searching and trying to find that rare special shiny card, I liked playing football but was not really interested in watching it. I supported Crystal Palace; it was my dad's team. I just brought the cards to try and fit in, hoping to make some cool friends, hoping someone would want to trade Gazza for two cards I didn't need, to be fair, two cards I didn't really want anyway.

If you're a certain age, you may remember recording the "Top Ten" on that radio cassette player of yours.

"Three, Two, One, press REC".

That's what everyone would shout. Ahhh, too late. You would either get a few seconds of the DJ talking or miss the first part of the song. It's funny what you can remember from years ago. I can remember quite a lot about my childhood and my early years. I had a great childhood.

I was born in Hong Kong back in good old 1976. I think we lived there for about a year: mum, dad, and my annoying older sister. She was born in Germany about eighteen months before me. Mum kept the house and looked after me and my sister. Dad was in the British Army, that's why we were in Hong Kong, Kowloon. I don't remember any of it, unfortunately, but I do have some pictures of the street I used to live on. It looks like a cool place. Mum tells me stories of how I used to play with the cockroaches as a baby. How mad is that? Ant and Dec, if you're reading this, I'm free for the next season of I'm a celeb. Ok, I'm not a celebrity, but are any of them nowadays? If I'm honest, I also don't want to spend time with people who mock Mental Health for a laugh. It's not "Woke," I just believe somethings are funny, and some things just aren't. Mocking and taking the piss out of people with a Mental Health condition is not right in my book. How would you feel if I made a joke about your past? Having said that, I do still love the show. Also, I can't dance for shit, so don't even bother asking about that one. The only talent I have is singing a cracking version of "Hero" by Enrique Iglesias!

I would love to go back and visit Hong Kong someday. We have some friends who live in New Zealand, so maybe one day, use it as a stopover. I know my wife would like to go. My sister did a few years back, and she said it was an amazing place. She even got a photo outside the flats we lived in, where I was born. I was so jealous of her.

We moved around quite a bit when I was little, always different schools, hell, different continents. My very first memory that I can recall is eating salami out of a plastic bowl. It was some ridiculous late time of night or early morning, millions of stars in the jet-black sky. We are sat in the car, ready to go on the biggest thing I had ever seen, a massive roll-on roll-off ferry. I have no idea where it was taking us or even where we were, but there I was, sitting in the back with mum and dad in the front.

Dad's driving with me, and my sister sat in the back. She is sitting on the right with me to the left, both of us holding plastic bowls with slices of peppered salami in them. Twenty feet away is the ferry, docked with these massive ropes hanging off the end, waiting for all the cars to drive on board.

I can remember a basement full of massive stuffed toys. Life-size lions and hippos, lots of stuffed toys. Bendy buses in Germany were fun, the way they twisted and turned; I loved standing in the middle section, turning and twisting around. I remember the van that used to come around. You would buy your shopping from it: fruit, vegetables, and sweets. It was like a mini corner shop but on wheels.

I've got scars, lots of scars, too many of them. I reckon I could give Sgt Martin Riggs a run for his money. The Olympic swimming pool in Berlin was the first scar I think I ever got, one I can remember anyway. It had these massive stone steps, like seating in a huge Roman amphitheatre. I fell over and smacked my head. It hurt.

I lived in America as a child; it was amazing and the happiest I have been in my entire life. It was totally awesome. We would catch lightning bugs in glass jars and go water-skiing on the rivers, flying over Newport News Naval Base in little light aeroplanes and looking at all the war ships and carriers sitting in the middle of the estuary. I loved flying. It was so much fun. When I was a kid, you were able to go and sit in the cockpit on the commercial flights. With a view out of the cockpit windows, looking out at the sky all around you, the clouds just floating there surrounding you. Night times were an amazing experience, the lights of the towns and cities below, a proper bird's eye view. All the stars, hundreds, thousands, tens of thousands of little twinkling stars. I would sit in the captain's seat and pretend to be the pilot with hundreds of people sitting behind me, not knowing a child was flying the plane. There was always that pre-boarding discussion between my parents about where to sit.

"Smoking or Non-Smoking?"

"Smoking"

That's the reply mum always gave.

"NON-SMOKING! I am not spending the next eight hours sat next to fag ash Lil. NON-SMOKING!"

Dad was a total anti-smoker, but only because he had given up himself, of course.

I have family dotted all over the United States. My auntie and cousins live in Mount Pleasant, Pennsylvania, and they get bears in the back garden! My auntie lost her husband many years ago. He was a soldier in the American Army and saw conflict in Vietnam. I have never met him, but I was always told that he was a different person when he came home. He developed PTSD and took his own life, a bullet to the head, I believe. PTSD, Post Traumatic Stress Disorder, no one really knew what it was. In fact, I thought it was just something soldiers got!

We would visit my aunt and cousins from time to time and go ice skating and fishing on the frozen lakes down on what we called Aunt Daisys farm. I got thrown in the cow's manure pit one day, some sort of revenge by one of my cousins for locking her in a cupboard or something like that. I really wish I could remember more about my life, but unfortunately, I have these massive holes where everything is blank. I would love to have known what I did to deserve a manure bath.

The East coast winters were so magical; the trees would be covered in layers of ice resembling an ice sculpture. Huge icicles as long as your arms just frozen in time, the occasional drip, drip, as the sun's rays melt away their existence. Snow and lots of snow, the lakes would be frozen solid, and you would have to cut through the ice with a huge drill to go fishing. We went sledging after a particularly heavy snow storm one afternoon. I was bombing down a massive hill next to the house, waiting to fly over a gigantic mound of snow. I had no fear back then. I was hoping to get some good air off this wall of pure white fluff heading my way. I didn't realise there was a brick wall inside of it, *WHACK*. I somehow managed to knock a single brick clean out of the wall with my forehead. The local town's doctor had to come round and stitch my head back together on the sofa. It was great. I got a dollar bill and a lollypop.

If you have ever seen the National Lampoons films, you would understand that was us. The family car was a green station wagon. Loaded on the back was a trailer tent, and that's when our American tour began. Disney World, Kennedy Space Centre, NASA, and the Wild West. Las Vegas and the Grand Canyon, we went travelling for months all around the United States. I've sat in Elvis Presley's car and met Jaws in real life. I've watched country and western at the Grand

Ole Opry, and I still love listening to country and Western music to this day. I love a bit of John Denver.

"Country roads take me home. To a place I belong, West Virginia. Mountain mama."

I love it, but not quite as good as Willie.

"You are always on my mind."

I can imagine me and Willie Nelson getting together, having a smoke, and singing that together. That would be a dream come true, the best song ever.

One night, we were trying to find our destination, an AKA campsite in San Francisco. We must have driven over the Golden Gate bridge half a dozen times looking for it. That's the night we came across a baby hammerhead shark someone had caught. They had placed it in a massive red cool box to show people before safely returning it back into the water. A hammerhead shark, for God's sake, just laid there in a foot of water in a massive red cool box. I can still see it staring at me. It was amazing to see.

America was crazy, always an adventure to be had. Sometimes, I would sit in the front of the Griswold mobile, surrounded by cases and cases of music cassettes, all in their black briefcase storage boxes. I was in charge of finding the songs that dad wanted to listen to and then loading them into the tape deck of the station wagon, hundreds of country and western tapes.

Have you ever been horse riding in the Rocky Mountains? I have. Driven through a plague of locusts? Seen the aftermath of a tornado? Been there and got the T-shirt. I've even been caught up in a 6.4-magnitude earthquake. It's a weird experience when the ground starts to move, doors opening and closing all on their own, the curtains swaying. One day, we were trying to find a nice sunbathing and swimming spot; the heat was relentless, and we could all do with a dip. It might have been in California; I cannot quite remember. Wow, the beaches were so overcrowded. We came across a secluded bay, and all ran into the sea to cool off from the midday sun beating down. It turns out we had a lucky escape; this man came running over after about ten minutes, waving his hands like a mad man. Shouting at us to get out of the water, they had only been pre-baiting the area for sharks since the morning! I imagined they were bigger and maybe a little scarier than my little friend in his little red cool box. These things were probably more like Bruce!

We went travelling for months, either sleeping in the trailer tent or just a normal tent on the ground. You would often feel the snakes crawling under the ground sheet, and I'm not talking about small ones. You could get massive blocks of ice from the vending machines, and I would race my sister down hills sat on giant blocks of ice.

We did stay in a few motels along the way from time to time. I remember this one motel we stayed in; it might have been in New Mexico or around that area. It had a swimming pool, and that was great because it was hot. I was being chased around the pool this afternoon. I'm not sure by whom or why, but they were closing in on me and fast. Right, what are my options? I keep running, and they would catch me, or I could jump into the water, but they would still catch me, maybe drown me, and I can't swim that well just yet. I still have my orange armbands on. My escape routes are very limited. I've got it. I can run onto the diving board and jump back to the side. They will think I'm jumping into the water and I can get away. So, it's one giant leap for mankind, and WHACK! It didn't really work out as I had planned. I jumped but didn't quite make it. My chin smashed on the pool side and split open so much my dad said you could see my teeth. I remember jumping, but not much more after that. My dad had to hold my chin together. It was busted up so badly. The motel had to drain the swimming pool because of all the blood. I even refused to visit the hospital. America was ace. We would drive for hours just to do our Sunday shopping, a chance to visit Chucky Cheese and McDonalds. It was a very rare treat back them and nothing like the corporate world you see today.

"Bring back Ronald McDonald."

The thing I miss the most is Long John Silvers; I loved that place. It really was like an old-fashioned pirates hideout.

I developed croup as a child and had to spend time in an oxygen tent at the local hospital. Unfortunately, it wasn't my first visit. I had to have my tonsils out there, too. I was on the operating table, and this female nurse placed a black mask over my mouth and nose.

"I want you to count backwards from five to one."

"Five, Four, Thr…. ZZZZZZZ".

Croup felt horrible, every breath you take thinking you're going to die, desperately hoping the room full of steam was actually doing something. That's where I first started hating needles. I can recall the doctor saying to me.

"We have to give you an injection. It's only a tiny needle!"

Well, to me, it looked like a knitting needle, just like the ones my nan used to use. It was massive. It is like calling a massive person tiny. I hate needles now.

The rest of the American family lived in Washington, DC. Mum's brother had something to do with the Jehovah's Witness Church, and he had the biggest house ever. It was like the White House. It was so impressive. It was a huge mansion, and on the top floor was a gigantic auditorium with row upon row of theatre-style seating. Mum and dad left us with them for a few days, so our uncle took us to the local supermarket, where we were allowed to buy a toy each. Dad, being in the Army, I wanted some plastic toy soldiers and a plastic gun, but this wasn't allowed, so I settled on some plastic dinosaurs. That evening, we had to sit in the back of the auditorium surrounded by hundreds of other people listening to a service or speech about their beliefs and what God they believe in. I don't have a problem with any religion or faith, but as a small child, gosh, it was boring, and I just couldn't wait for mum and dad to come pick us up.

I love America. It holds a very special place in my heart, happy times. I was even selected by my elementary school, Lee High Elementary, to sing "Oh say, can you see" and read the Pledge of Allegiance for morning assembly over the tannoy system. Dad didn't want me to do it as I wasn't a Yank. I shouldn't be singing and reading the Pledge of Allegiance. I'm English. But I did, and I loved it.

"Oh, say what you see, by the dawns early light"

I had a proper, deep American accent then. I didn't want to leave America, but I was also quite excited to be returning home to the good old United Kingdom.

I have been fortunate enough to visit the US a few times since moving back to the UK and even won a competition where I spent three days, all expenses paid. It was on a golf trip, all thanks to Red Bull's Final 5 competition. I stayed at the Pinehurst Golf Resort in

North Carolina. We had the privilege of playing courses Eight, Four, and Two, all for free. With caddies wearing white overalls and a green hat, I felt like I was a professional golfer on tour. It was an amazing experience.

The American dream had to come to an end, so we boarded the plane, and I made myself comfortable for the long journey home.

"Non-Smoking"

We moved around for a few years to and from different Army bases. I loved it and had some great times discovering what we called Lost Valley, just farm fields and a stream in reality. It was magical. I would spend hours in the valley playing and trying to catch fish in the stream, building dens, and climbing trees. Doing secret raids on the farmer's fields, we even played in grain silos. Please don't do that if you're reading this book; it's extremely dangerous, and you can die!

It snowed really heavily one year, and dad taught us how to build a snow cave in the side of the bank. We used to go up and fly in C130 Hercules aircraft, flying over the countryside with the back doors opened. You can see the whole countryside zipping away underneath you, people walking around like ants. Your vision just tunnelled through the back doors, staring in amazement. The defining noise of the Fat Alberts, I loved it. I was still doing stupid things and being reckless, building the biggest ramps I could and jumping over the local kids on my BMX bike. It was good that they would lie down behind the ramp, and I would bomb down the road and just take off, flying through the air. I loved my Pogo stick, jumping onto walls and up and down stairs. I would spend hours and hours just jumping and bouncing around. I joined the local Cub Scouts and even became a

Sixer. My arm was bulging with badges, Scout Jamborees, and campfire songs.

"Oh, you'll never go to Heaven on a piece of glass. Because a piece of glass might cut your finger."

"Ging gang goolie goolie goolie goolie watcha ging gang Goo. Ging gang goo".

I learned to drive around the airfields in an old Army Land Rover and drove massive articulated forklift trucks in the hangars. Dad even brought home some surplus Army paint, and I helped paint his car all with a paintbrush, standard issue Army green. I think it was an Austin Allegro. That's when I started to become a little shit, nicking the odd sweet from the local shops, nothing major, one hundred and ten, no more and no less, always one hundred and ten.

"I'm not going last. I went last, last time, so that's not fair."

I would grab a small packet of Frosties and shove them in my jeans pocket, that sort of thing. Come on, admit it. We have all done it. I'm sure most of us have got that special glass we stole from the pub, another one to add to the collection.

I had lots of friends on the camps. We would go and play around the military base, thinking we were spies on a secret mission. Marching around the parade square in our little squad singing songs like.

"So, you wanna be in my gang, my gang, you wanna be in my gang. My gang."

We would go off exploring old abandoned anti-aircraft positions and play football on the soccer pitches. I stood on this hole in the ground one day. It was only the size of a 50-pence piece by the halfway line. When I moved, the ground erupted with wasps. I ran for my life with this swarm hurtling towards me, the immense sound of hundreds of wasps buzzing all around me. My left arm was covered in them all, trying to get a little piece of my flesh. A woman came running out of the house. She could hear me screaming, and she swiped them away with a tea towel. I hate wasps, bloody horrible things. I will never forget what happened that day. One day, some friends at the camp got bored, so we decided to break into someone's shed. Well, to be fair, the door only had a latch, so technically, it wasn't breaking in. Jackpot, we hit Aladdin's cave. It was full of Army gear and, the best part, ration packs, shelves full of ration packs. We were hungry. All we needed to do was heat them up.

It was only meant to be a small fire. Well, that's how it started anyway.

"Don't worry, it's not that big. I can put it out."

Me trying to be the hero. I don't know what liquid it was, but let's just say it didn't put the fire out; we ran, and we ran fast. The fire brigade was called, and the shed fire was finally extinguished.

After I severely denied any knowledge of the said incident, I decided the best thing for everyone would be to disappear. I hatched a plan to run away. I had a money box shaped like a ten-pin skittle. It had a white top with a blue bottom, a Halifax bank savings account gift possibly. I removed the top and emptied my life savings out, and with my bags packed, I headed to the NAAFI. Right, what do I need to live on my own? Frozen Oven Chips, check. Several packets of Cherry Flavour Tunes, check, and a jar of Cockles in Vinegar, check. Off I trotted. I knew where I was going, down past the married quarters out towards no man's land, down by the Officers Mess. There was a small tree I used to play in; I would play soldiers, pretending I had a machine gun firing at the enemy aircraft flying overhead.

The Army Camp was first built as a training facility for fighter pilots in the 30's. It was even used as a training school for pilots during World War Two. I used to think I was shooting them down. The German pilots are racing overhead in their Focke-Wulf aeroplanes, their equivalent to the UK Spitfire. I loved the Focke-Wulf planes. It was the closest thing to a swear word I could say as a kid without getting into trouble. I loved Airfix models. For hours, my dad and I would sit around the dining room table, building them. We used to go visit my Nan and Granddad from time to time, and opposite their house was a little shop that sold Airfix models. I loved going there for a new toy. It was a lovely house with so much land outside looking over an old abandoned quarry. Nan didn't speak much English; she couldn't even read or write, but she was always shouting in Italian. I loved visiting them, mainly to fill my pockets with sweets. There was always a bowl of fruity bonbons on the sideboard. Grandad used to spend hours in the garden growing plants. He loved his little seeds and watching them grow. I would quite often join him in watering the plants in the greenhouse. I would sit on the slim shelf units, and he would talk to me about tomatoes. He grew so many plants the greenhouse was covered floor to ceiling with black and terracotta coloured plastic plant pots. The garden was always bursting with vegetables.

The Focker's flying overhead. I'm making the sound of a machine gun in my head right now, and I'm firing on the enemy planes circling around me. There is a row of houses in front of me, but one of them is different. It was rebuilt in a different style after being hit by an aircraft during the Second World War. I was shooting the planes down again, watching them crash into the house.

"Come get it, you Focker's."

A huge fireball, BOOM. The rat tat tat of my machine gun blasting away.

I'm there again right now, reliving that experience. Sitting on a branch buried deep in the tree with both my arms out in front of me, both hands grasping the anti-aircraft machine gun I'm currently holding. Moving it around from left to right, then back again. Shaking my hand whilst I'm making the sound.

"RAT TAT TAT, RAT TAT TAT"

Try it, go for it; imagine you're there right now with me. I can feel the breeze. I can feel the temperature dropping as the sun disappears behind the soft white clouds floating in the sky. I love to reminisce about the good old days.

I had run out of Tunes on the trip down, in all about seven packets. I had eaten all the cockles and drank the sour fish juice straight from the jar, like a shot of tequila down in one. I was getting hungry because raw semi-frozen oven chips didn't really taste that nice. It started to get cold, so I headed home. Not a single person had noticed I was missing. It was still early, though. I told my parents and mum moaned that I had emptied my money box. Dad said I would have been easy to find. Just follow the trail of sweet wrappers.

Living in the Army Camps was such an adventure. I used to sneak around the hangers and march like a soldier on the parade square.

"I'm the Leader"

I especially loved going to the Sgt's Mess with my dad. I loved disappearing into the snooker room and playing a few frames by myself. Dad would often get some shotguns and bullets from the armoury, and we would head down past the airfield and shoot rabbits together. He has taught me a lot over the years. Shooting and hunting, fishing, and how to survive out in the field.

I did make a few friends over the years, but I was always a bit of a loner. Yeah, I would go and play hide and seek with the rest of the kids singing.

"Eenie Meenie Miney Moe"

Playing cricket and football, sometimes Kirby and Knock and Run. I was never the one that used to get invited into their houses. The friends I did make weren't real, just odd people like me, really. People that didn't fit in, for whatever reason that was.

We didn't have a lot of money. Believe it or not, the USA was paid for thanks to the British Army. Most of my clothes were from the market. Supermarkets didn't sell their own clothes back then. I remember going to Stow Market one day with my mum. I loved going out with her. It felt like a huge adventure. It did with both of them, to be fair. We went on the bus to get a new pair of jeans for me. It turned out that when we got home, they were skin-tight, and this was before skin-tight was a thing. My God, I cried, but we couldn't afford another pair, so I had to wear them. Unfortunately, it was an accident, I promise. I was playing at the bottom of the road, having a stone fight. It was horrendous when a sun-baked dog mess looked like a stone, and you went to pick it up. Oh well, good for the immune system. I totally forgot I had £2 pocket money in my new jeans. One of my enemies just shouted that they had just found a £1 coin on the floor.

Soon, realising I had probably thrown them at someone. Your pockets were always bulging with rocks to battle your way out of a corner. It started to get dark, and when the street lights came on, it was always time to get home. We did push it from time to time, but we never went far from the bottom of the road. Legend said there was a paedophile who lived in the house at the end of the street, down by the garages. He liked to pray on small children and babies after dark. I slipped over on some gravel and put a hole in my new jeans. Mum was not impressed. She thought I had done it on purpose just to get a new pair that fitted me. Sadly, that wasn't the case. I now own the first pair of skin-tight jeans with holes in them. I would be considered a trendsetter nowadays.

Trainers, don't get me started on them, GOLA. It's funny, but I would quite happily wear them now as I see them as retro, but believe me, back then, they were just another reason to have the piss taken out of you. In my later years at school, one of my uncles popped around and gave me a pair of brand-new trainers. He had brought them, but they were too small. I really didn't want them only because I had never heard of the brand, but I was told I was having them. I just knew that the next day at school, I would have a ribbing. I reluctantly put them on in our PE class, but to my amazement, all the cool kids couldn't believe it LOTTO wow.

"Cool trainers"

That made me feel great. I was one of the kids at school that could hang out with anyone. At school, I could spend time and talk to the geeks. Likewise, I could spend time playing football with the cool kids, the ones who always had Nike trainers and Nike jackets, Nike rucksacks. I was so happy one day when one of the cool kids called me mate. We were riding around the block on our bikes, and he had to go home.

"See ya, mate."

I had a smile from ear to ear on the journey home that afternoon. We were actually coming back from work together. The local market needed help to take down the metalwork, all that box steel that made the market stall. We got paid £4 to help. There was a really creepy man that used to run one of the stalls. You would be on a step ladder unhooking the beams, and he would come up behind you and prick you with something on the bum. I have no idea what it was, but I was on the receiving end of it quite a few times. That day, I cycled home and heard the word "Mate". That was an immense feeling, a feeling I had never had before.

In the school fancy dress discos we used to have in the assembly hall, I would get dressed up in some massively oversized Army gear my dad gave me to wear. School non-uniform days were great. What the hell am I going to wear? I don't own anything with a brand name on it. I am going to be getting called.

"Loser"

All day long, I blame it on some idiot at Lloyds Bank. If you opened a savings account, you got a free jumper. Lloyd's Bank green and black, guess what I got to wear. I was off sick the next day. I mixed water with some Cheese Puffs, nice and mushy, then threw some on my carpet. Proceeding to make a vomiting noise, proper Goonies style, sick day.

You would always get picked on for the clothes you wore or the trainers you had. People you thought you liked calling you.

"Loser"

All the time.

I did average at school but didn't really try hard. If I'm honest, I have always thought I have dyslexia in some way. I have problems with my bs and ds; I am always getting them mixed up. The only way I can remember it is this. I know how the word bed is spelt; it starts with a b and ends with a d, so if you look at the word bed, it's a bed shape, with a headboard and footboard, easy, really. Also, my spelling is atrocious. Every time I try and spell the word once, it always comes out as wonce. I have no idea which witch is which or wear their and they're need to be. I attended Special Needs classes at school with extra tuition in reading and writing, that sort of thing, just another reason to be picked on.

"Here comes Special Needs."

That sort of thing. I could not tell you the order of the letters in the alphabet until I was in my late teens and only knew the order of the months of the year because I could say them in French. The only reason the other kids didn't pick on me more was because I was a good goalkeeper due to my size. I never knew how the cool kids could kick a ball so well. I just gave it a good old toe punt with my size 12's. I have always been tall, and with long legs and long arms, I would fill the goal, which makes saving balls a little easier, and the fact my hands are like shovels. It didn't really help that my ears are massive, though.

"Big Ears"

It was always my favourite or…

"When you getting them pinned back?"

I was one of the best at rugby at school and cricket. I loved playing rugby; it was a way I could keep control. I was better than the Nike brigade. I took my frustration out on them on the field. Always a good hard tackle when required. I was that good at rugby, and I even had trials with Gloucester Rugby Club. I so wish I had continued. Unfortunately, I ended up getting banned from the school team. In one match, I broke someone's nose and busted someone's ribs!

I hated reading, so it wasn't great when we had to do an essay at school. Read three books from the same author and write an essay about it all. My worst nightmare, I managed to find some short stories. I can't quite remember who by, but the stories were about 8 pages long. I'm sure one was something to do with a sea turtle. I love reading now, but I haven't done it for a while, and to be honest, I don't know why because I used to really enjoy getting lost in a good book.

We had a school trip to France for one year. I was so excited that I was able to go. It was a trip, canoeing down the Ardeche then, followed by a week's camping on the South Coast. We all had to write four names down, people we wanted to share a tent with. No one wrote my name down, so whilst everyone was having fun, I was stuck in a single tent on my own.

My dad caught me cycling along the main road one day. The very long way round to get to school, battling the traffic on a very busy road. I told him I was getting more exercise so I could get fitter and be better at sports. The real reason was that the bigger boys from the other secondary school would be waiting for me in the mornings and after school, there to beat me up because they fancied a girl who lived at the end of my street. What would you have done in my situation? Imagine it: you peer around the corner, the same routine you do most days, hoping that they are not going to be there today.

I can see them. It's three of them, this time about 40 yards away, staring down the old railway track, blocking my way towards school. It must be true; the bigger boy's brother had joined the hunt. I was told he had been in prison and that he really wanted to hurt me. He had form. The tattoos on his face and down his neck seemed to confirm this and the nickname of a dangerous creature. I ran the half mile home and grabbed my bike. I think I will take my chances with the traffic; the exercise will be good anyway. I was threatened with a knife wonce. It was at the open-air swimming pool. I had just got back from a family holiday to Corfu. I had one of those plastic sun lounger float things. Some bigger boys stole it from me. On their way out of the swimming pool, I was given it back, all split open, ripped to shreds. Not a single puff of air left in it. One of the kids pulled a Swiss army knife out of his pocket. You know, the little ones that folded up, they had a handy pair of scissors and a toothpick on them.

"If you tell anyone. I will slit you!"

I was only about thirteen at the time. There was not a chance I was going to talk. I didn't want to get hurt, slit open like my lilo. I'm just standing there holding this floppy thing in my hands.

"I won't tell anyone, I promise."

I never returned to the open-air pool after that. It was not until a charity fundraising day that I helped out many years later. I found myself working in the fish industry and took an eight-foot shark along to the fundraising BBQ. Guess the weight of the shark, then we cut it up and cooked it on a BBQ. The shark in question was a Porbeagle. Google, it would certainly make you think twice before going into the sea in the UK.

I was glad when school days had finished. Most people I knew were heading off to sixth form or college; I just couldn't wait to leave, get a job and start earning some money. I would be able to buy my own things, games, and nice clothes that all the cool kids wore, maybe something with a logo on it. The world would be my oyster. There will be no stopping me. Well, sort of. It was only a matter of time before I joined the Army. My dad was high up in the Army, medals the lot. I never quite knew what he did in the Army, but he was always away. He would be away for months at a time; I would never hear from him. Sometimes, he would be away for three months, then come home for two days before departing again to some far-flung place for another month or so. It was always the expected thing for me to join up and follow in my father's footsteps. Being in the forces was a family tradition. My granddad was a Navy man on the submarines and HMS Ark Royal.

Due to my dad being in the Army, we had to be careful in life and be safe. He was a potential target for terrorists. We would always look under the car before driving off, checking for bombs. I found one one day.

He went off to work one morning but left the car for some reason. I was off fishing, and as I was walking past the car sitting on the drive, I noticed a bag underneath. I called his workplace and had to get him dragged out of an important meeting. This was an emergency.

"Dad, I think there's a bomb under the car. It's like a rucksack under the exhaust."

It turned out to be some maggots and fishing bait one of his best mates had left for him. The crazy part is he was a local CID police officer. That's what life was like back then, when all the troubles were happening, anxious stress always worries. It's crazy some of the things he has been through. The worst that I know about is probably the Riyadh compound bombing in 2003. Mum and Dad were both caught up in that one!

I only recently found out he was checking out a port overseas somewhere in the Middle East. I believe it was Kuwait. The car in front was blown up by a grenade. One minute there, and the next, a grenade tearing through it. They did a quick 180 and got out of there. He doesn't know if it was a targeted attack on him or the military. Maybe the terrorists got the wrong vehicle, or in fact, that was the intended target. I don't blame them for not staying to find out. People just don't realise the things that go on in this world. I'm not some sort of conspiracy theorist or anything like that. I just look at the facts and make my mind up from there. I don't think people have landed on the moon. There are too many anomalies with it all. Just google the Van Allen Radiation Belt. It wasn't the Titanic that sank but its sister ship. The ship was sunk on purpose for the insurance money. Just look at the propellor! It went down and sank in the wrong place; it was going to rendezvous with another ship in the mid-Atlantic, where everyone would be rescued. Well, like I said, life is crazy. Maybe I am. Who really knows what goes on in the world?

Ice Skating on Aunt Daisy's Frozen ponds was so much fun. Pennsylvania around 1983.

Our Griswold family car and trailer tent. We had so many adventures travelling around America, I loved it. Growing up in America was the best time of my life.

27

The Winters were Magical. The Trees covered in Icicles as long as your arms. America was Ace!

I loved going up in light aeroplanes and flying over Newport News Naval Base. Seeing all the battleships in the estuary.

Here I am sat in one of Elvis Presley's Cars. I think this one was from the film "My Blue Hawaii" I'm not the biggest Elvis fan though.

Four Corners Monument. The borders of four different States meet here.

Utah, Arizona, Colorado and New Mexico.

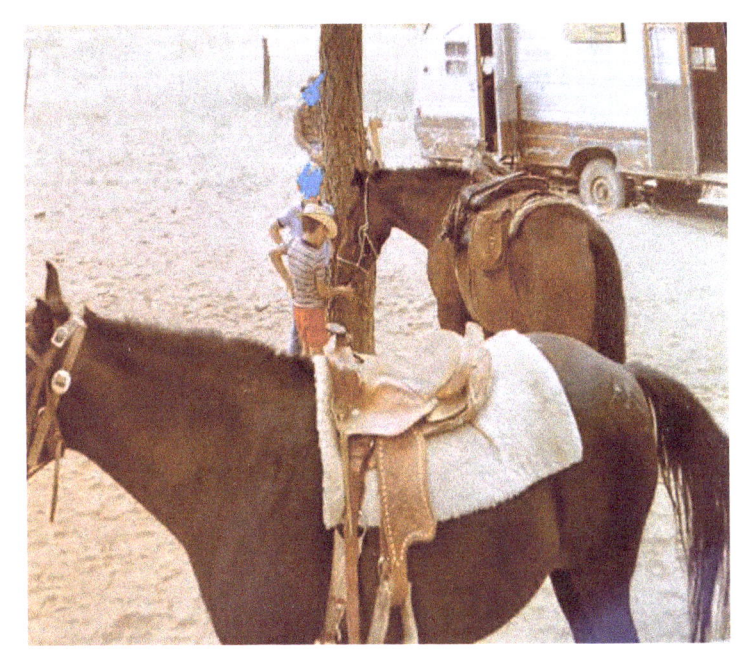

Getting ready for a trip. Horse riding in the Rocky Mountains. Bloody horse tried to throw me off! That's me in the cowboy hat.

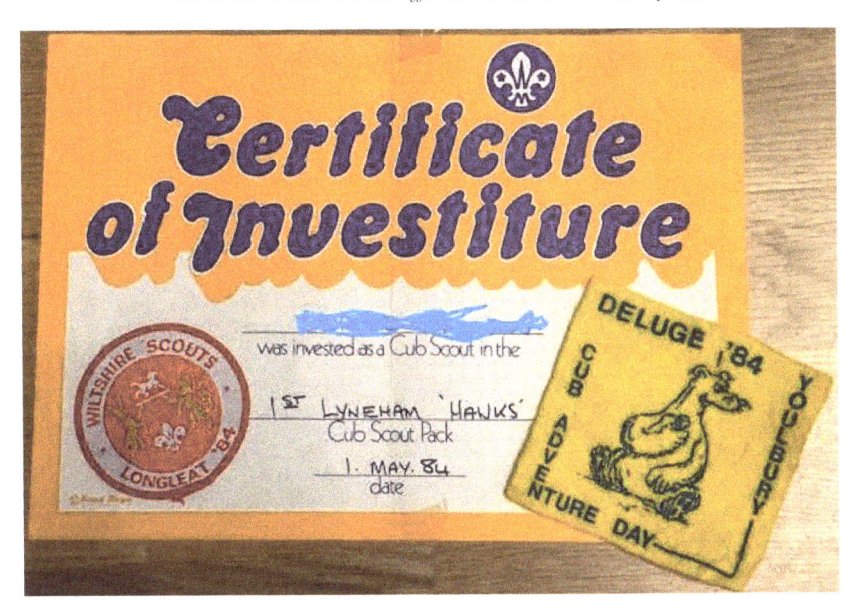

I had a whole arm full of Badges. "Dib Dib Dib" Bob a Job week was so much fun.

"You're gonna need a bigger boat"

Universal Studios, Orlando with Bruce aka JAWS.

Chapter Two
Tea with Two

In the early '80s and '90s you didn't have an app on your phone. Believe it or not, kids you didn't have a mobile phone at all. I know how crazy that sounds. Mobile phones did exist,, but they were about the size of an XBOX. You had to have a good job or plenty of money back then to afford one of them! The telephone was attached by a cord to the wall. In our house, it was in the hallway on a little coffee table.

Our generation was the best generation that ever existed. Generation X, we played out till the street lights came on and drank water straight from the hose pipe. If you wanted to know where we all were,, you just looked down the street, looking for the mass of bikes thrown on someone's lawn. That's where our squad would be. We spent hours wandering up and down the streams and rivers trying to catch Snotty Gogs, more commonly known as Bullheads, who hid under the rocks. The Stone Loaches always preferred the faster-running water. You had to be a good angler to catch one of them. Should we follow the river under the old railway bridge, that would be a huge adventure. We never did, though; it was a very long, very dark tunnel, and we could cut ourselves on something sharp or, worse have a leg chopped off. We came up with so many excuses no one would admit the truth. We were scared the Bogey Man would get us.

We had just enough technology to make life fun and interesting. The kids nowadays, it's too much technology. Yes, I'm sure you all have many friends, but how many of you actually have friends? Proper friends, friends you can go on a bike ride with, friends you can go and kick a football with. Not the online ones that prefer to hide behind an avatar and ask for pictures of you. It's a dangerous world on that web, so just make sure you really know that friend you have been chatting to, and if any of them ask for any rude pictures, then please tell someone straight away. These people are not your friends.

Sadly, not everyone in the world is nice, and wishes you peace and happiness!

After getting seven grades C's and two D's, school days were finally over, well, so I thought. The truth is I didn't enjoy school. For me, the highlight of my school career was leaving. As I walked out on that last day with half a dozen signatures on my shirt, a couple of girls in my year stopped me.

"Did you know you were voted the boy with the biggest dick in the whole year!"

I had no idea. Then I got egged by one of my school bullies, ginger twat!

Not having school in my life felt very strange to me. I even went back for a few weeks; yes, I was one of the people Mr Gilbert was talking about. I helped out in the PE department, refereeing the school football matches and that type of thing. The school kids would always moan at me, though. I didn't really understand the offside rule very well. I knew I couldn't do this forever, so it was time to look for a job. I had to go to the job centre. All the available jobs were written on an index card and placed on a metal rack under its section: Warehouse, Cleaners, Admin, you get the picture. You would have to get the reference number from the card and then go to see an advisor. They would give you the details of the employer for you to contact. I hit the jackpot at a local care home. They were looking for a part-time member of staff to make the residents breakfast. Simple things like cereals, tea, coffee, two slices of brown toast, butter, and marmalade, that sort of thing. After the breakfast run was completed, I would have to spend time in the kitchen on dishwasher duty. Then came setting the dining room tables. Placemats and cutlery, glasses, and every place setting would have a burgundy paper napkin in the shape of a bishop's hat. I had to do so many of those damn things a day, twice as many if I had a day off the following day. I would quickly swap into my tight-fitting burgundy suit jacket and dicky bow tie, serving teas and coffees to all the residents. I knew what everyone wanted, including their favourite biscuits, and I knew exactly where everyone would be.

I really enjoyed this time of my life. I was meeting real people and having a real job. I loved talking to the residents and listening to all their stories of the past. What life was like in their olden days. Olden days that make me laugh. I dropped my son off in town a few months back for a music festival. He was fourteen at the time. He's a very sensible lad, so I have no fear for him. Well, I do, but kids do need freedom. When I picked him up, I was asking if he had a good time. Obviously, the answer was yes. I had given him a tenner to grab some lunch with his mates and asked what he had eaten.

"Subway 6-inch sandwich with extra meat and extra tuna with crisps and a drink it was over £8."

I remember when you could get a meal for about £3!

Anyway, he had fun, so that's what makes me happy.

"So, what sort of music did you listen to?"

"A lot of old stuff, really, like No Limits and stuff like that."

Bloody old stuff, how times have changed. That song was a banger when I was into clubbing.

The best part about the job at the nursing home was it was part-time. I had to start work at about 6:00 am to get ready for the breakfast shift. It was excellent as I finished at noon. I would race home and get my fishing stuff before heading down to the local lake. What could be better, working in the morning, than fishing in the afternoon? To top it all off, you got paid. It wasn't much, really, but I had cash, although most of it went on new fishing equipment. I was good at fishing; in fact, I was very good at fishing. I have fished for several fishing clubs over the years. I can't quite remember the date, but I was technically the second-best intermediate fisherman in the whole of England in 1992. All those many hours chasing and catching Stone Loaches had paid off, and I finished 2nd place in the National Fishing Competition. The Intermediate Nationals held on the River Thames at Marlow, I caught 21lb of Chub all on the tip with a block end feeder, double bronze maggot on a size 16 Kamasan B520 hook. A large feeder bursting with bronze maggots. All caught under a huge willow tree growing on the far bank, a good chuck for any angler, let alone a sixteen-year-old. I wish I had carried on fishing as I could have ended up in the England team. I went to see them once In Spain, Toledo, in 1999. I even did an interview for Sky Sports shouting.

"COME ON KIM"

Behind England international Kim Milsom's back, I don't think he was impressed. The camera crew had told me to do it, to shout like I was attending a darts match. On the final day after the fishing match had finished, and Dad and I were walking down the bank heading back to our bus. We came across Bob Nudd, the England three-time Individual World Champion icon. He looked gutted; he had lost out on the individual championships this year, and someone by the bridge had beaten him. I told him what the guy had really caught and that he had won his 4th title. I have recently been chatting to Bob Nudd about it, and he can remember that moment.

I loved fishing. I used to fish amongst the current England Team Internationals when we were all young and used to beat them no matter what the venue was. If only my dad had owned a lake, still no point in holding a grudge. I was so glad Dad used to take me fishing as a youngster. I'm reconnecting with it again after decades away. The times we would sit on the bank fishing away, my sister used to come too, but she would always catch more fish than me. Even when I would cry, and we would swap swims, she still caught more. I would consider myself a top angler, but even I blank someday, so a little patience is required.

In the early days, we fished lakes and rivers, canals, well basically anywhere. Fishing is a great hobby for everyone, no matter what ability. Learn the sport, and talk to other fisher peoples. Watch YouTube videos, just get on the bank, and enjoy yourself. It's amazing for your personal well-being and Mental Health. I love fishing again, and a good friend of mine has even reintroduced me to sea fishing. It's been great, and I've caught some whoppers. I haven't been sea fishing for donkey's years. I did it a few times as a teenager, then again at a works society I was involved with. We would go out wreck fishing from Exmouth, fifty miles off shore.

I was driving on this particular trip. We got to Gordano services, and I fuelled up the minibus, bursting with rods and equipment for the day ahead. Then we headed south. We made it almost to the end of the slip road before the van conked out. I didn't know what diesel was. I just used the green hose like I always did! We returned back to Swindon on the back of a recovery truck and missed the tide.

I've just started fishing again. It really helps with my Mental Health. I have even started fishing the lake I fished as a junior before my life went to shit. It holds a special place for me now, a place before the bad times. It is full of fish and birds, and the wildlife is stunning. I don't care if I don't catch anything because it's so relaxing, just being sat next to the lake listening and watching. It's only a two-minute walk from my new house, so I try to get around it when I can. I wish I could get around it more than I do, but I'm sure when it's safe, I can.

Even though I had my fishing and my job and the Army looming, I still didn't have many friends, not real ones anyway. I was friendly with all the staff at the care home, though. I made friends with my boss Tony, he was the head chef, he was funny. All the kitchen staff were funny and nice. I liked them all. It was great to finally have people around me that liked me and had fun and played with me. We would have a laugh spraying each other with a water hose attached to the oven, then rolling kitchen towels up and flicking each other. I liked the night shift staff, too. They had to let me in the building in the mornings so I could start my shift. I thought adulthood would be hard work, but it didn't seem that way. One of the night porters would tell me stories of them spending their evenings in the resident's lounge having sex with each other! He would put a word in for me if I wanted to have sex with one of the female night porters. Apparently, she loved it, young meat. He would sort it out for me. He was a great guy, Alwyn. He would always greet me in the mornings and let me into the building. I would park my bike down by the bin store. He would always be outside smoking when I arrived, always handing me a cigarette before shift, always finding time to chat whilst we finished our fags. He would spend hours helping me with the breakfasts. He was my mentor and taught me how to use a toaster, how to make coffee, and what Room 2 liked every morning. We chatted about anything and everything. He loved listening to stories of my childhood, growing up overseas. Stories of me ice fishing and skating on frozen ponds, Disney Land, and Universal Studios, what games I loved to play. I loved talking about my childhood. It was such a happy time for me. Unfortunately, everything has to come to an end though. So, one day, that was it. My head was shaved, and Dad was driving me down to Arborfield, the Army base that would be my home for the next 22 years.

I walked down the pavement towards the building; my ears were cold, and the top of my head was tingling. I went through the left-hand door as it was propped open. It really was like a scene from a US military film. I headed in through the door and turned left to walk up the stairs.

"Come on, move it, get up the fucking stairs now, move FUCKING MOVE IT."

Someone was shouting at me, and they were loud.

"Yes Sir."

"SIR, I'M NOT A FUCKING SIR you see these stripes. Get up the stairs. FUCKING NOWWWW."

I shit you not, that's exactly how it happened; I honestly feel like my life is a weird version of Forrest Gump's, except my box of chocolates is full of them coffee ones.

To me, it was pretty pointless to drop your stuff and get your head shaved. Mine already was, always had been for most of my life, but it still got cut anyway, and I had to pay for the privilege.

Army life was tough all the early mornings and late nights, never any rest, ironing your kit and folding it neatly, only for it to get thrown over the floor ten minutes later. Oh well, start again. We have to get it right. We need to try and sleep before the fire alarms go off, normally between 2:00 am and 3:00 am. We would never beat the time set, though. Someone would always forget their boots, more beastings. You knew as soon as that fire alarm went off in the middle of the night that you were in for an hour of pain, already sleep-deprived and wanting it to be over. We had to be up at 5:00 am, so a few hours kip would do us all good. We would scrub the toilets for hours, only for an officer to come in wearing muddy boots. Proceeding to clean them in that perfectly polished porcelain sink, taps you could see your reflection in. The officer would just stand there whistling away to himself, dirt and mud being thrown everywhere, very little care and attention being paid to the mess he was creating all around him. Thanks for that, don't worry. I will clean it up for you.

Not all Army life was bad. I loved the shooting. That was fun. We would spend time on the gun range shooting at cardboard targets with a two, two conversion on an SA80 machine gun, even using some smart new technology, the SUSAT, and the not-so-technical penny depressor.

Camping outside was great fun, spending two or three days and nights out in the sticks. We would patrol around the woods at night, fighting the enemy, always on guard. We knew they were out there; they had come every night so far. Our call sign was Whisky, India, hoping someone would reply Mike Papa, and if they didn't, that's when the fighting would start. We cooked ration packs on heximine stoves and had a plastic sheet to put over our heads at night, a bit like a canopy. You would have to dig a little hole in the dirt to sleep in with a companion to huddle up to and try and keep the body warm. Not me, though, still the odd one out. I guess that's what happens when there's not an even number. It felt like being back in school all over again. In the end, it was the fitness I struggled with. Imagine getting gassed in the morning, coughing your guts up, trying to get the burning sensation out of your eyes. That sensation you get when you rub your eyes after cutting up a hot chilli it's just a hundred times worse. Not being able to breathe and gasping for what little breath you can. Every breath burning away inside your throat, spit dribbling out your mouth. All this was followed by a good few hours of double marching on the parade square. The afternoons getting beasted around a gym for hours and hours on end. What's that, a five-mile run to finish the session off? Don't mind if I do, thanks.

I'm sure my parents were disappointed with me when I came out of the Army after only a few months. The reality for me is it was a massive relief. I was too young and way too immature to be a part of that life just yet. I totally disagree with 16-year-olds being able to join the Army, or if they do, the first six months should be training on how to iron or make your bed, just learn to be a grown-up.

It's proven that the human brain does not develop fully until the age of about 25. That's a few months of my life I'm not going to get back.

I do have so much admiration, though, for the likes of Ant, Foxy, Billy, and the gang. I met Ant Middleton at one of his book signings. I waited for ages in line, just to be first in the queue, although I'm still waiting for him to make good his promise to me! Our country owes you all a great deal of gratitude for keeping us safe, even if people don't know what you do or how the world really works. Thank you all.

The end of the Army was not all bad. They had not been able to find a replacement for me at the care home. There I was, back to it, tea with two sugars. I was so happy when I found out the staff had all remained. I could go back to spraying Tony with water from the oven, I could catch up and chat to my mate Alwyn, and this time, he's going to speak to the lady on the night shift for me. It won't be long now.

We started to build up quite a good friendship. He only lived a two-minute walk from my house, and as he worked nights and I finished at noon, I would spend hours around his house playing Dungeons and Dragons board games. The idea was to beat the Red Gargoyle. I loved playing board games, and Dungeons and Dragons was one of my favourite cartoons. I couldn't believe my luck one day when he bought a new computer. It was the same as mine, an Amstrad CPC464 complete with all the latest games and quite possibly the best joystick you could imagine. It was like something from a jet fighter. There were several buttons on the top, the sides, and the bottom it was immense. I felt like I was Maverick flying an F-14 Tomcat.

I would spend hours playing upstairs in the spare bedroom, The one over the garage, next to the toilet that leads down the open stairs. A right turn into the living room and dining room, like an L shape, a small door at the bottom of the stairs that leads to a small porch area. The large living room window looked over a small garden onto the open green space where all the kids used to play. The fireplace, the shelves on the right where he kept his special things. Alwyn would come in from time to time asking how I was and if I was enjoying myself, the answer was always.

"Yes".

Once, when he was leaving, he placed his hand on my shoulder.

"Stay as long as you want. I love seeing you enjoy yourself."

He loved the fact I was having so much fun.

I stayed late one night, and why shouldn't I? I was an adult, after all. The other month, I was shooting machine guns in the British Military!

I had been drunk before; it was at a bar my dad had built in a hangar on the Army Base, "The Dragem Inn". I worked behind the bar on the opening night. I must have been about fourteen. All my dad's squaddie mates and soldiers he looked after were there. I was working behind the bar serving drinks. I'm drinking a pint of lager, watching my dad coming over, telling me to

"Go Steady Son".

He walked off with half his drinks order, so I downed the rest of my pint, then grabbed all the slop trays and emptied them into the pint glass. Proceeded to down that as my dad came back for the rest of the drinks he had left behind. Dad thought it was the same pint I had just demolished. I got a lot of cheers from the lads. I felt so proud being around people having fun. My dad's smile at me said it all. I'm sure Esther Rantzen would have had something to say about it. Anyway, as far as I was concerned, it was better than playing a game of Freckles!

It wasn't neglected. That's how things were in the 80s. I do not see that I was neglected as a child, and growing up to me, I had a great childhood. There was always an adventure to be had somewhere. Going fishing with my dad and spending time with my mum. Constantly fighting with my annoying big sister, life was great. Sunday nights playing a family game of Monopoly and watching the late Jim Bowen hosting Bullseye, bet they win the speed boat. Cilla trying to match make, then always wondering what Graham had to say about it all. I went to bed every night listening to Graham Torrington's Late-Night Love show on the radio.

It was Carling. I didn't know it then, but I can remember the black-and-white can. I only had half of it before feeling really dizzy and strange. I ran upstairs and threw up in the toilet bowl. Lager wasn't for me. You best avoid it from now on. Alwyn drank sherry and lots of it. I couldn't stand the stuff it stank. It was quite a relief when he brought me vodka. Vodka and coke that was nice. I had always liked Coke.

I was invited around his house one Sunday afternoon; his wife was cooking a Sunday roast. I had never met her before. She was always sleeping or working. I believe she also worked in an old folk's home in Cirencester. They had guests for lunch, by the look of it, two adults and a child, a very small child. Alwyn had invited me round to play on some new computer games he had just brought. Off I ran upstairs to my little room over the garage whilst everyone was sitting around the dining room table and enjoying their Sunday dinner. I think it was chicken.

I broke the law; I knew I shouldn't have, but I did. I knew drugs were bad, but Alwyn had been smoking them for years, and it's never done him any harm. It was resin back then. Sometimes, he would have proper weed, but mainly the black stuff. I would spend hours and hours around his house drinking, smoking, and playing board games. Defending my ground against that Red Gargoyle. I loved the feeling of being high on cannabis; it felt good, drifting off for hours on end with no cares in the world. Just me and my mate together, having fun.

I was living a normal life. I didn't have any worries, I had a job, I had money. I had a friend, oh and alcohol and drugs, lots of drugs.

I've always loved fishing even from an early age. USA around 1982.

A huge Conger Eel 44lb. I'm 6'1. They grow 8 times this size!

I think my school report is bang on. Toledo 99 where Bob won for a 4th time! Disney Land was $9, and a card from my friend Larry when I was in Hospital with Croup. Only the second time for me on a horse. My Chinese Birth Certificate top left.

Form Tutors report. Robbie appears to be having some social problems this term. He has difficulties, quite often, with other pupils both in and out of the classroom. This inability to cope with others is now giving cause for concern.

SPECIAL EDUCATIONAL NEEDS DEPARTMENT
ANNUAL REVIEW

Name ....[redacted].... Form ... 2 ... No. of sessions per week ...[redacted]...

VOCABULARY DEVELOPMENT — [redacted] is capable of using complex vocabulary in his work but this is not as evident in his writing as it should be.

SILENT READING / READING ALOUD — [redacted] can read fluently but he needs more practice at adding the appropriate expression when reading aloud.

WRITTEN WORK — [redacted] has some very good ideas, but he seems to experience some difficulty in developing these to their full potential. He needs to learn how to plan and structure his work more carefully so that this problem is avoided. He has a script handwriting problem.

ORGANISATION AND USE OF WRITTEN MATERIALS — [redacted] enjoys using reference books and other written material for research. He would benefit from more practice in note making. He is able to follow written instructions well.

SPELLING — [redacted]'s spelling has improved over the year although he still finds some words a problem to spell, in particular more complex words. Also, he has a tendency to be rather careless with the spelling of basic words. He must learn to check his writing.

AUD/VIS DISCRIMINATION / HAND/EYE CO-ORDINATION — Not applicable

SIGNED ...[signature]... DATE ..17/7/89..

N.B. Where pupils attend the S.E.N. Dept for a limited number of sessions per week, or period of time, it will not always be appropriate to make a comment in each of the above sections.

What a fantastic name for a class of people that need extra support and tuition!

Chapter Three
The Royal Connection

I have had the greatest of pleasure meeting some of the Royal family. The first time was inside Buckingham Palace. My dad's a hero. He was given a medal by the Queen; God rest her soul. He saved the world.

He was overseas during the first Gulf War. I think I know most of the story and what happened, but I can't quite be sure,, so I have decided to leave it out. I know it's got something to do with the Turkish Government and planes. If my dad didn't do what he did and when he did it,, then full World War 3 could have broken out. I can get married in St Pauls Cathedral, so that's pretty cool. My dad even met Prince Diana once. We have a picture of him waiting in line, ready to greet her. All you can see is Princess Diana staring at my dad with a huge smile on her face. My dad thinks she fancied him!

Mum's amazing, she really is, but to be fair, you would have to be an amazing person to put up with my dad being gone most of the year, keeping a home and looking after us kids. I often remember helping around the house when Dad was away, running to the NAAFI to grab a box of OMO soap powder. OK, that bit was a joke, but I thought it would be funny. It's a coping mechanism of mine to laugh, sometimes at shit situations.

Mum has always treated me like her little boy and still does to this day. I have so much love and admiration for her, so I kind of let her get away with it. She always makes me laugh when I go and visit them both. She will always chuck me a few hundred quid and tell me to have a nice break.

"Just don't tell your dad. He doesn't know I got this squirreled away."

It's all a nightmare, to be honest, as dad's just the same. He will always pay for everything. Tickets to the waterparks, dinner, and trips to the golf courses.

"Just don't tell your mum I've given you that. She doesn't know."

I love my parents with such a solid love. It's unreal, and I know that it's given back to me tenfold. However, I will not have anything to do with stews or gnocchi again, no thank you. I love the relationship my parents have. You can tell the love they have for each other is solid, and it makes me happy knowing they are out there looking after each other.

Alwyn used to work behind the bar at Cirencester Polo Club. He gave me a job there working behind the bar, too. This was massive. Not only was I mixing with the Royals once again, I was getting paid £80 for a shift.

You would always know when they were coming, the Royals. The police would do a sweep of the Polo Club with sniffer dogs looking for explosives or guns. I guess looking for a potential threat to the Royal Family. To me, terrorists were easy to spot. They wore a vest full of bright red sticks with the letters A.C.M.E down the side of them. I often wondered why they never looked at me and thought, he looks a bit young to be working behind the bar, but they didn't. A little ginger-haired kid would be playing with his dad, watching the other Polo Club members on their horses galloping around. I never really got to watch much of the polo. It was always so busy.

Alwyn had a system, make sure you know the prices because if the drinks order is under £20, you have to add 10% to the bill. If the order is over £20, then you add 20%. There is no such thing as contactless payments these days. Cash was king.

I swear I have lost count of the number of Pink Gins I have made over the years; it was never sold readymade like it is nowadays. Have you ever wondered what that small bottle of Angostura is? Well, 4 drops of that stuff added to gin and tonic. That's what makes it a Pink Gin.

I loved working at the Polo Club. It was great, £80 a shift, and as much vodka as I could drink, we were always on it. Alwyn always made sure I had a drink in my hand.

A huge explosion knocked me for six one day. Alwyn had thrown a vodka bottle on the floor; he told me it was to hide what we were drinking.

"Don't worry, I will put it down as spillages."

The bottle would have been empty at the time, just glass to collect, although that was a task in itself. The bottles were always the gigantic ones my parents used to save small coins in. Remember the ones that you would often shake all the money out of just to nick a quid's worth of 5p and 10 pence pieces, then run to the corner shop with one hundred and ten sweets on the way?

I remember the day like any other trip to the Polo fields. We met at his house and cycled to the Polo grounds, the same as we always did. We opened the bar and got ready for the day's events. We would always get there really early before anyone else, and once the bar was set up, it was time to start drinking, time for a smoke.

The day went normal. I was chatting to Jilly Cooper about her latest film she had just done and how she was going to write me into her next book somehow. I'm not sure she ever did, though. If I'm honest, I've never read a Jilly Cooper book, so I'm sorry about that.

A group of girls ordered some bucks fizz, but when I tried to charge them £12 a glass, they said.

"No Thanks".

I ended up having to drink them for a forfeit at the end of the shift, all six of them, down in one, one after the other. They were kept cold on some sort of frozen plate to the left of the bar. I got a bonus that day for all my hard work, £120, that's the most I had ever earned in one day and not bad for a young lad. We locked up, then grabbed our bikes and headed off through the woods back home, the same route we would always take down the long track, through the impressive iron gateway, down Cecily Hill, and past the Castle, which is also where the open-air swimming pool is.

We didn't ride far that day. Alwyn said he might go and have a play with himself in the trees. He told me to go and play with myself, too. We dumped the bikes, and off I walked down a track he had shown me. He left me on my own, and yes, now writing this, I'm ashamed to say I went into the woods and played with myself.

I got back to the bikes, but he wasn't there anymore. The bikes were, but he wasn't. I looked down the track a little, trying to find where he had gone. There he was, standing behind a tree, half hiding with his head and shoulders leaning to the side. He was looking at me, smiling and gestured for me to walk towards him.

"Turn around."

He walked up behind me, my back against his front, then placed his left hand on my crotch.

"Nice."

That's the only word he used, whispering it into my ear. I can still smell his breath, the fags, the booze, the sherry. He walked around me and knelt down in front of me. He proceeded to unzip my trousers and started to touch me with his hands and with his mouth. I just stood there, totally silent and completely still.

"That's enough for today. Let's go home."

He declared before zipping me back up. I didn't know what to think or what to do. I went round to his house, we drank, we smoked, we played board games, Dungeons & Dragons, we were special friends now. I had to keep it a secret, though, as no one would understand how two people so far apart in age could love each other so much. They just wouldn't understand. He sealed it with a kiss on my forehead, then held me tight.

"Even if you told people, they wouldn't believe you. They would try to ruin our special friendship."

Life carried on as normal after that. Working at the Polo Club was great. I had lots of money and could buy even better fishing stuff and nicer clothes. I bought a pair of shoes with the logo "Kickers" and an "Ellesse" shirt.

There was a back room in the bar. It was like a barrel store with an old wooden door, kind of like a stable door, opening up to the outside world. All the small kids used to hang around playing by the tree next to the door. A huge mighty Oak Tree with a little security hut to the side. I worked on the security side there for a while, checking people's memberships, making sure there was no trouble, and looking out for a terrorist. It is mad to think I was a skinny runt of a lad, still lanky with big ears, acting as security for the rich and famous Prince Harry and Prince William, our new King. I guess I one could say I have been part of the Royal Protection Team. However, this may be a little bit of a stretch though.

That mighty Oak Tree was always a meeting point for the small kids. Parents were just glad they were out of the way so they could enjoy their Pink Gins unhindered. The kids were always playing and having fun. Alwyn was always giving them drinks and crisps and inviting them into the bar area. He really was a lovely, caring man. I really looked up to him. My life was normal completely normal.

I would start my shift at the old folk's home, meeting him outside in the mornings. The cigarettes had now been replaced with a joint. He would take me into the toilets and do things to me. He would take me into resident's bedrooms whilst they were asleep and do things to me. In their bathrooms, sometimes in their hallway by the door. I guess he got a thrill from them watching us. The residents did not know what was going on. Most of them didn't even know their own names. On breakfast duty one day, Alwyn was standing in the doorway. Tasmin Archer was singing about Sleeping Satellites when he asked me if I had any favourite residents, and yes, I did. Some of the old people were lovely. I remember one particular old lady; unfortunately, she was very old and frail and not quite with it all. I used to love spending time with her. She was always an early riser, so I would take her breakfast in personally. We would spend five minutes chatting about anything she wanted. Sadly, her health declined, and the dementia had gotten worse. Mrs F sadly passed away; she was my favourite. I can still remember her to this day. I think I know her grandson.

Alwyn told me he had a favourite once; I remember his favourite resident. He didn't go into any details, but the smile on his face had said it all. The signs were all there; I just didn't know what I was looking for. We didn't have social media back then, and only four TV channels to watch. The only television we watched was Phillip Scofield in the Broom Cupboard, Grange Hill and the A-Team. We didn't hear about paedophiles. They only existed in myths and legends. We just spent our time playing, watching what little children's TV there was at the time. Seeing Rolf Harris playing with his digeridoo, singing about tying something down. Always wondered what lucky little boy or girl Jimmy would select this week. Access to media as a kid was very limited, and there was nothing in the Beano that suggested otherwise. We knew that paedos existed and what they did, but that was it. Every street would have a legend of a paedophile who lived close by, ready to pounce on babies when they were asleep. Ours was the guy at the end of the road simply for no other reason than he used to moan at us kids for kicking the ball against his garage. It's perfectly reasonable now that I'm an adult.

    I spent a lot of time around Alwyn's house in the evenings, getting so messed up. God only knows what I have taken over the years. I can't remember half of what went on, and I don't like not knowing.

Dad receiving his MBE. Inside the Grounds of Buckingham Palace. The Turkish Government also wanted to give him their equivalent to the MBE but he was not allowed to accept it for political reasons. He is my hero.

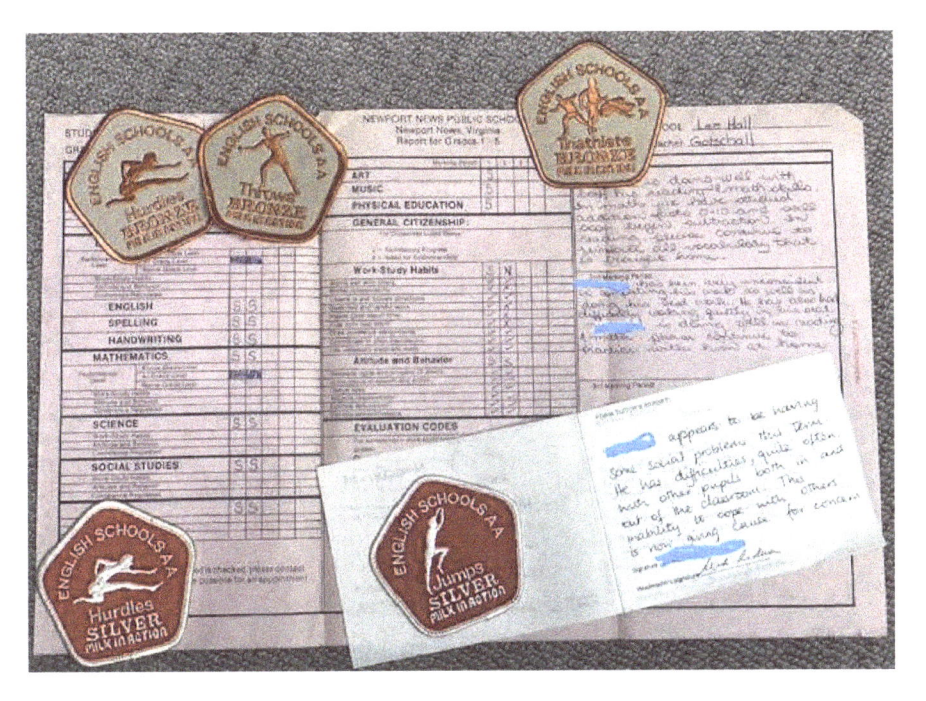

I loved sports as a child. My dream is to watch England v New Zealand at Twickenham. Then, get mortal with Tindell and Zara.

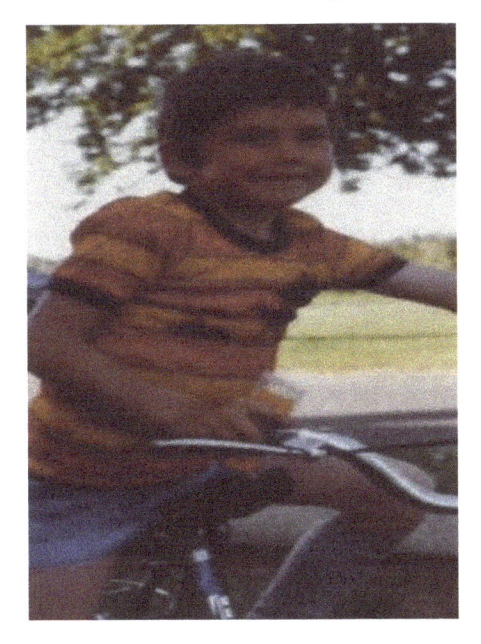

I loved Riding my bike as a kid. The amount of Air I could get off a ramp was mad. I Could make Clint Eastwood look hard.

**Chapter Four
And They're Off**

I was so lucky that Alwyn had a job every year at Cheltenham Races, Gold Cup Week. He got me a job there too. The first time we went down, I was given a green and white striped waistcoat complete with a green bow tie. Cheltenham Races, you can't get much bigger.

We drove to Cheltenham in his little beat-up white car, a Nissan Sunny or Micra, I think. We stopped somewhere in Cheltenham and into a bar full of his male friends. He introduced me to loads of different people. He must have been so proud of me. I would have a few cocktails, and then off we would go to the races, ready to clock in for my shift.

When we got to the racecourse, we met up with another guy, another of his friends. It was obvious they knew each other by their greetings, a good hug and an embrace. I struggle a little here because I can't quite remember what happened at the races. I only worked there a few times. I remember being walked around through lots of rooms rammed with partygoers having fun, lots of men and women shouting, and people singing. It was such an amazing atmosphere. I remember people used to come up to me and just shove money into my hands. They must have got lucky, I guess.

I remember a drive home one night after the races had ended. It was really early in the morning. We were coming up to a junction on a country road, and he stopped the car and started laughing.

"That's where another of my friends got naked and was dancing around in the middle of the road a few years ago. He was so wasted!"

Flashbacks, a memory that's all I get; my counsellor tells me I have managed to bury these traumatic events for so long, and that's why I'm getting them exploding to the surface now. Visions of the trauma and abuse I suffered all those years ago. Although I can't remember everything that happened, and to be fair, I should be thankful for that. I can remember enough, though, not everything, but enough.

There's a dark room. It's dimly lit. Someone is standing in the corner in a black suit and tie next to a lamp. I don't know who he is, but he looks a bit like the man I met when I arrived, Alwyn's friend. A small bench-type stool is in the middle of the room. I'm naked from the waist down. I'm lying belly down over the bench with the vivid green stripes of my waistcoat, and my trousers and boxers are down around my ankles. I knelt over the bench, looking behind me. Alwyn is in the room with me, and so is someone else, a man. I can hear them talking. I don't know what they are saying, but they are having a conversation.

You would always be sure to come home from the races with a good couple of hundred pounds. I brought a Diawa Amorphas Whisker stick float fishing rod. It's hard not knowing, but everything has a plus side. Maybe sometimes it's best not to remember.

I started to think this wasn't right, but what could I do about it? I would go around his house when he told me to. We would smoke weed; I would get £50 to go buy something nice, plus a small bag of cannabis to take home. I had started to distance myself. I found another job, full time and got away from the nursing home. Luckily, we moved home soon after, so he was on the other side of town, even more of a reason to stay away and not bump into him hanging around the estate.

Because I started to stay away from him, I didn't get any more shifts at the Polo Club. That's why I went and worked in the little security hut next to that big mighty Oak Tree. I was still mixing with the rich and the famous, still watching William and Harry playing with their dad. I certainly wasn't invited back to the Cheltenham Festival, so I'm back to being on my own. Not for too long, though. I soon got out drinking heavily in the pubs and nightclubs. Most nights of the week were spent down the pub gambling ridiculous amounts of cash on the fruit machines, trying to win £6 in beer tokens. Fridays, Saturdays, and Sundays in the nightclub smashed beyond belief, sleeping on pavements in the winter out in the snow and waking up with a pavement pizza by your side. I started taking more drugs: cannabis, speed and half an ecstasy tablet. Please don't resort to drugs. Read Leah Betts' story. If that's not enough to put you off for life, I don't know what is.

I was a complete idiot for ages. The speed made you stay awake for days on end. The music in the clubs was amazing. Smacked off my tits, just banging my head around, incessantly chewing on Wrigley's Gum.

"No No, No No No No, No No No No, No No. Theres NO LIMITS"

God, I hope that was easier to read than it was to type. I bet you skipped it anyway and just sang it aloud in your head. I did many times. I'm forever doing that and have done it ever since I can remember. I sang songs in my head over and over. Hundreds of times, thousands of times. The same song, normally just a short part of it, constantly singing.

"No No, No No No No, No No No No, No No. Theres NO LIMITS"

Second verse same as the first.

"No No, No No No No, No No No No, No No. Theres NO LIMITS"

I hooked up with any girl who would have me, lots of pointless, meaningless sex. Friends, strangers, I didn't care, one night stands, you name it. My head was spinning. I didn't know what way was up, down, left, or right in them days. The bigger boys were still around, that was for sure, and for some reason, they still didn't like me. I would hide in the nightclub after it closed, refusing to leave. They would be outside waiting for me, ready for another kicking. I had to lie to the bouncers once. I was punched and kicked in the head by one of the local thugs, and the bouncers came flocking over. I was laid out on the floor, holding my jaw where I had just received a boot. I told them nothing had happened. I was so scared of what was going to come later, come closing time. No one likes grass, and I was petrified.

I still see them around the town to this day. The last time was a week ago. He was coming out of one of them cheap DIY stores. More weight around his belly, but still with a menacing look on his face, I dare not make eye contact, still too scared after 30 years. He might still recognise me and give me another kicking.

Sadly, I had a strange attitude towards sex then. For me, sex was something that just happened between friends. It didn't mean anything, just that you were friends. Brenda had taught me that about a decade ago, in the good old US of A. She was a neighbour when I lived in America. She taught me things, where things went, and how things happened. To me, this was all a normal life. I would often wonder when all the abuse was going on, why the other people I worked with did not want to have sex with me. They were all my friends, so I didn't understand it. I nearly asked the head chef one day.

"Why don't you want to have sex with me?"

I wonder what would have happened to my life back then if I had said them words. To me, I was asking a friend of mine why he did not want to have sex, for no other reason than he was my friend. Not because I was gay, not because I fancied him or anything like that. Friends have sex with each other, don't they? I just happened to have started my sexual journey at the age of about seven.

I sit here now wondering how Brenda knew what to do at such a young age, what she must have gone through in her own life to know what sex was all about before even reaching puberty herself.

I have read in a book that it's about understanding and trying to give forgiveness. Maybe Alwyn was the victim? Maybe he was abused as a youngster, maybe worse than my experiences. Maybe he thought it was perfectly normal to act in the way he did. Maybe in his world and his beliefs that, what he was doing was ok. Maybe I should forgive him for it all because he didn't know any better and that he was suffering too.

No, sorry, but I refuse to accept that. You knew exactly what you were doing, and even if all these horrible things that may have happened to you are true. What you did was calculated. It was manipulative. You orchestrated the whole thing to get what you wanted: the prized little kid. That little boy who came to work with you as a colleague, as a friend. You are the work mentor who taught me how to make coffee and what Mrs F liked for breakfast. Fresh out of school, a loner with no real friends. You knew I so desperately wanted a friend, a special friend who was thirty fucking years older than me. You used me as a plaything; you knew it was wrong, but you still did it anyway. Alwyn Clayton, I will never forgive you for what you have done to me.

Right, so here's the thing: I'm not really sure I should have said all that. I want this book to help you. And part of your journey might be forgiveness, and that is what you might need to do. We are all different. We all have different ways of coping and dealing with the situation. What matters is how you find a way through this; I'm still trying to find my escape route. If I can find a way out of this prison sentence that's currently in my head, then I can get through it. I just wish the water wasn't so hard to wade through. We all have ways of coping; we all have to do things to survive. For me, I was willing to do anything to survive this. I've been pretty much a functioning alcoholic for most of my life and an on-and-off soft drug user with a gambling addiction. That's how I survived for many, many years.

I lost fifty thousand pounds on a horse once, kind of. I had a plan, and it seemed like a good one. I bet 50k on a horse. I can't remember the name, but it was the favourite. Odds about 2/1. I typed the figure out on the computer and placed my bet. My thinking was, if my horse comes in, amazing, I'm going to move abroad. If the horse lost, I was going to kill myself. The transaction didn't go through, not enough funds in my account. So, I tried 40k, but still the same message: 30k, 25k, 20k. Ten thousand, Five thousand. When people say there is a price on your head, there really is. My life at that moment in time was worth £4999.99. I placed my 5k bet, but it still didn't go through, still not enough funds in my account. I wasn't prepared to go any lower and kill myself for less than five grand. I did have a nice conversation with someone from the bank's fraud team the next day, though.

I started to settle down after years of trying to find a stable relationship, and that's when I met my wife. It was at a New Year's

Eve party; I won't bore you with all the details, but we got together and bought our very first home.

Cirencester Polo Club Bar somewhere around the early 90's.

I have no idea if it still exists, but if it does, it needs to be torn down. Far too many young boys were groomed and abused here.

**Chapter Five
Something's Wrong**

Kids, what can I say about kids? I love my kids. It's funny, when I met my wife, kids were the last thing on my mind. If I'm honest, I never thought I would have any. I just knew the world could be a crap place. I remember the day very well. Me and the missus had been together for a while now, and we had bought our first house together, mainly thanks to my parents. They had sold up and moved full-time overseas. Dad was an expert in explosives of some sort and how to get things from one side of the world to the other. His services were in high demand. Mum and Dad had given me twenty grand, so with the money, I cleared my debts, and the rest was put down on a deposit for our first home. My wife fell pregnant after a few years together and another house move, all thanks to her parents this time.

We had moved back to a village we both loved and called home. My wife was huge. Honestly, the belly on her was gigantic. We knew it was going to be a big one. I didn't really know what to think or how to handle it. I was happy but scared all at the same time.

Due to complications at the birth, she was rushed into emergency surgery and had to have a C-section. It's a massive blur, and time flies by so slowly it's strange. I recall the doctor saying.

"Ohh, that's a lot of water!"

As it filled his boots, this was shortly followed by.

"Wow, it's a massive head".

My wife had been in delivery for days, hours, and hours seemed to go by. The baby was taking so long to deliver and had gotten stuck.

The doctors thought it had swallowed its own meconium, basically, its own poo. So, as soon as the baby was delivered, it was going to be passed to a team of medics. They did their checks, and it seemed like a lifetime before we both heard that first cry. It was an amazing feeling; a wave of emotions ran through me. Hearing that cry was the best thing in my life, and my little boy was born 11lb 1oz. You could hear all the other mums on the maternity ward talking to their husbands and friends.

"Hers was massive, Over 11lb!"

It's funny all the emotions you go through. Mine was sheer joy and thankfulness that everything was ok.

It would be another year's wait until my daughter was born. Again, a big one, just under 10lb. One of each, a boy and a girl, how wonderful. This time, monitored very carefully, the wife again bursting out of the seams yet again. A planned C Section this time, they knew it was going to be another whopper. We had always decided not to find out the sex of either child. So, it was so amazing to have Daddy's little girl and Daddy's little boy. I was made up, and my little bundle of joy had completed our family. Sadly, my wife ended up having an infection after the birth and had to spend a very lonely Christmas and New Year's stuck in the hospital on a drip.

I had started working the night shift at a local factory, and trying to sleep during the day was tough. Constant baby screams. It was almost a rest going to work. One night, I was walking through the factory. I have always known when my body hasn't felt right, and if I'm honest, I have always felt different. But on this night, I just didn't feel right. I was stressed, overworked, and tired constantly. So, what do you do when you don't feel well at some ungodly hour of the morning? Having a fag and a coffee seemed like a good idea, but in reality, it probably wasn't. We were due to go out with the kids and some friends the next day, so I went home for a few hours of sleep and then headed out for a day's adventure, some Thomas the Tank Engine trip the wife had planned. I woke up in pain; my arm was aching, and I had a toothache. After googling my symptoms, my wife decided the best thing to do would be for her to take the kids out alone. The mother-in-law would drop me at the doctor for a quick check-up.

My wife's parents have always been extremely supportive of us both and have given us so much support over the years. Even though we are now divorced and living separate lives, I know they still care. They still chat with me and give me the odd hug. It really helps.

My wife loaded up the kids and set off to meet Thomas and friends, with friends. I jumped in the mother-in-law's car and was chauffeured to the quacks. That was in the days when you could walk into the doctor and get an appointment. Not like nowadays when you have to book your sickness months in advance and get your life story questioned by a receptionist. I talked to the doctor about how I was feeling and what my symptoms were, so as a precaution, they sent me to the hospital for some blood tests. Ok, I have to admit it: it was quite nice and relaxing on a hospital ward rather than being out with young kids screaming all day. I was just too tired. I just needed to sleep. I was sent to a ward whilst they ran my bloods.

A doctor came over a few hours later, and she explained that they had analysed my blood and that one of my levels was high. My Troponin levels were very high.

"You have had a heart attack."

I was only 34 at the time. With that, another three doctors and medical staff turned up and loaded my bed with various pieces of equipment. A doctor dressed all in green carrying a huge rucksack full of life-saving equipment and drugs with a defibrillator swaying in her arms.

"We are transferring you to the Cardiac Care Unit."

I looked at the doctor.

"So, all this equipment is that just in case I die on the way down to the ward?"

"Yes, it is."

Came a short, sharp response. As I was being wheeled onto the Cardiac Care ward, an older gentleman greeted me. He must have been in his eighties. I later learned he was in for a triple bypass, his second one.

"Ohh, a younger one this time".

"Just trying to keep the average age down."

Came my reply, complete with a warm, welcoming smile and the obligatory wave to the rest of the inmates who were awake. To be fair, there were only four of us in the room, with a nurse station watching over our every move. Listening incessantly to all the beeps and the bongs constantly going off around her.

I was sent for a procedure where they insert a wire into your leg and follow your veins up to your heart. The surgeon was watching the TV screen above my head. Eventually, the wire snaked its way around my body, following the subway system of veins till it reached my heart.

"It's full of clots and almost completely blocked."

He informed the other doctors and theatre staff present. Seconds later, my vitals started to drop, and they had to insert a special balloon inside of me. It was linked to my heart in some way. Every time my heart took a beat, the balloon would inflate to help. I had to have it in for 24 hours. That's the most uncomfortable thing I have ever experienced; you can feel this thing deep inside of you pumping away, up and down, over and over. I had to be monitored by a nurse for 24 hours. Under no circumstance was I allowed to move. Just laid there on my back for 24 hours with this thing inflating up and down with every breath. The feeling and pain it was horrendous. I thought with every painful breath that I took, an alien was going to pop out of my chest. So, I cried and got very upset. They had to give me morphine to calm me down and get me off to sleep.

It took me a while to get over the operation and to try to get myself right again. Something was always nagging me, though. I kept telling my cardiac consultant that I was still getting chest pains. They didn't believe me and just kept saying they had fixed me. I was actually sent to see a shrink. What's the point? All they want to do is blame everything on your childhood. They simply thought because I was only 34 years old, it was all shock, all in my head. I couldn't see the point in a shrink; I knew what I could feel. It's my body, and I've always known my body. After several seasons with the head doctor talking about my childhood and more meetings with the surgical team, my consultant said to me.

"Look, I think this is all in your head. We have fixed you, but because of your age, you are struggling with what's happened. The only way we can reassure you is to have another heart operation, and we can prove to you that you're ok. You have been fixed."

So, under I went again. I Had to be knocked out this time as I just couldn't face it. I nearly died there and then on the operating table the first time and even Jesus only got one return, so what chances have I got? The scariest thing about it all is you are awake watching it all in real-time; it felt like a dream playing out in front of your eyes, all on a 50-inch-high-definition TV. I'm not doing that again without being knocked out, would you?

I woke up in my bed in the recovery room, and the doctor was talking to another patient. When he had finished, he came over.

"We have found that the stent we inserted last time has failed, and your body is rejecting it. So, we have no option but to send you for open heart surgery. You will need to have a heart bypass."

Not the greatest news that you want to hear. On the plus side, I was right, just like I told you. In fact, the most disappointing part of that experience was that they had forgotten to put a catheter in me when I was on the table having my angiogram. I had to be fully awake whilst some male nurse inserted this thing down my shaft. Sorry, but no form of lubrication prepares you for such horrible experiences in life.

It would be a few months to wait to get in and have my chest cut open, and trust me on this one. It is also not a good idea to sit and watch YouTube videos on the procedure you're going to have. That time was so stressful I kept thinking I was going to drop down dead at any second. I would go into the kid's bedrooms late at night when everyone was sleeping. I couldn't sleep just thinking about everything, over and over and over again. I would give them both a kiss and tell them that Daddy loves them and say goodbye, just in case I didn't wake up in the morning. I would sit there on the end of their beds, gently stroking their foreheads. Desperately trying to hold back the tears, hoping to still be here in the morning. Praying to God that everything's going to be alright.

"Please God. I don't want to leave my babies."

Christmas came and went, then the New Year, and it was finally the 4th of January 2010. I called the hospital in the morning just to make sure the operation was going ahead. The green light was given, and off to Bristol, we went. With all the paperwork signed and risk assessments completed, a nurse handed me some pills.

"If you need to go to the toilet, then you need to go before taking these pills. Once you take them, you are not allowed to move out of your bed."

I opened my gob and chucked them in, grabbed the cup of water, and took a few deep gulps, and that's it. I cannot remember a single thing after that. I came around in the recovery room with wires and tubes coming out of every hole possible. Beep Beep Bong, Beep, Beep Bong. This young nurse came over and said hello. She told me that everything had gone well.

"The only thing I have to do is to remove your chest drains."

I didn't think much of that; I was too zoned out still. It's a bit vague, but I think she almost climbed on top of me. She was only a short oriental woman. It felt like she grabbed hold of this tube sticking out of me and yanked it out. I could feel this thing moving, almost creating a vacuum, a slippery slurping sound as it was being pulled out from deep inside my body. I sat bolt upright, almost fighting against it, gasping for breath, grabbing onto my chest.

"My God, that's horrendous. That's the worst pain I have felt in my life."

I gasped.

"I have to do the other one now".

My heart just sank. It was so painful, and thank God for morphine. You could self-medicate; every time you need some relief, you would press a button, and it would automatically inject you with the good stuff to keep the pain away. Yes, safety measures are in place so you don't overdose. Once you press the button, it will time out for a while. You can't get another fix, not for ten or fifteen minutes anyway. I was told off by my nurse for getting through too much.

"Try reducing the number of times you need to press the button. You're going to be in a lot of pain after what you have had done. It is a major thing you have just done."

It was obvious I was in pain, so much pain you just couldn't hide it. Every time you moved, the gasps and the groans. Physically holding onto your body, your arms wrapped around your chest, locking everything in position, and the fact that I've got a Dirty Great Big Bandage on my chest soaked in blood, it was a bit of a giveaway.

I was chatting with one of the doctors one night and asked him if they ever had any problems with the wire breaking in some way. The wire that they use to join your bones and your ribs together after they cut your chest in half with an electric rip saw.

"Yeah, there's a gentleman next door. We can't get his chest closed. Just keeps bursting open all the time."

I hoped he was joking.

In the old days, well, what I would consider old days. You would have to spend weeks lying in a hospital bed recovering from an operation like this. Nowadays they try to get you to move as much as you can and to get mobile. They were going to send me home after day four. Sadly, that wasn't going to happen to me. Unfortunately, I got an infection following my bypass and had to stay in for another few weeks.

I was getting really annoyed that I could not get up to go to the toilet. I was hooked up to so much equipment, but I needed a wee and was sick and tired of trying to use one of those cardboard bowls. I would always spill some. It was late at night, and I didn't want to bother the nurse sitting at her station watching over the four of us. Beep Beep Bong, Beep Beep Bong. I thought I could do this; I've seen the doctor do it on another patient. I stood up and grabbed the stand next to my bed. I took hold of my neckline, several tubes and wires feeding into the hole in my neck, and started to untwist one of the tubes. Blood just started gushing out. Whoops wrong one. It was spurting everywhere: on the walls, on the bed, the floor. Every time my heart beat, it shot further away, a bright red stream of blood spraying everywhere.

"Help"

I shouted, and the nurse ran over and reattached me. I don't think she was very happy, and the place looked like a murder scene. Talking about murders, I did think I was going to be murdered the day before. I was in a recovery ward with the three others. An elderly man was to my right. I think he had Alzheimer's or something like that. He had a visitor last night, and I'm guessing because of his illness; he told his guest that I had attacked him the night before and I was trying to kill him. He talked about how I had inflicted all these wounds on him and that I was a danger in some way.

I was laid in my hospital bed hooked up to all sorts of equipment and machinery, but I could hear him telling this guy how I had attacked him. Obviously, I was in no state to do a surprise midnight attack on the old boy, and even if I was capable, then why the hell would I? I'm not a monster; I'm just some bloke who's ill, that's all. Can't you see me? Hello, I'm here, the one with the blood-soaked bandages wrapped around me. The one with all the tubes and wires sticking out of pretty much every hole. I'm easy to spot! Anyway what am I going to use as a weapon, a cardboard container with half a kilo of piss in it!

I think his guest thought otherwise, though. He threatened to beat me up and hurt me. He was very abusive and started shouting at me. The nurse had to calm him down, and security was going to be called if he didn't. There I was, stuck in a hospital bed with wires coming out of every hole possible, fearing I was going to be attacked and beaten up with no way to defend myself. I was scared for my life. Cheers, mate. It was a pleasure meeting you, too.

I was in the recovery ward doing quite well, and they were saying they may discharge me soon. I called my wife and said don't worry about bringing the kids all this way to see me, as I'm getting out tomorrow. That's when the infection came, and I had to spend another few weeks inside a further few weeks recovering. I had to have another chest drain fitted as I had started to get a fluid build-up in my lungs. I was sent for an x-ray to determine the best spot to insert their new pipework and drain my lungs. The radiologist marked a spot on my back just below my shoulder blade for the doctors. Later that night, a doctor came and sat beside me with a few injections to numb the area, then a small incision through my skin. He pushed the tube into my body, and then it stopped. He couldn't get it through my muscles. He kept trying and trying, but it just kept getting stuck. He made the cut wider and pushed harder. I was screaming the place down, calling him every name under the sun. This went on for about an hour with so much pushing and pulling. Eventually, he had to give up and called another surgeon who was just about to go into theatre but got called away to assist. The new doctor cut a lot deeper and pushed a lot harder, and after another half-hour battle, he gave up, too. Let's try again tomorrow, he declared. I couldn't wait for the morning to come and have that all done again.

He turned up around about 11:00 am, but I hadn't seen him before. Cool as anything, he walked up to my bedside and spoke.

"I'm here to put a drain in you."

I told him about last night's performance, but he wasn't aware. I questioned him on his ability, his career, and his success rates.

"Pretty good."

He said, so I let him have one go. I had a few pricks with the numbing stuff and a small pushing sensation that I didn't really feel.

"All done."

"What, that's it, you've done it. Why were you not on shift last night?"

In total, I was away from work for a whole year, and even then, it was a phased return to work. It was a long recovery. All the way through this, my wife had to look after the kids, with me being the biggest one, and all whilst still working a full-time job. The pressure must have been incredible. I do admire her for everything she has done and continues to do, in fact. She kept life going, but it was not much of a shock that after a year or two, we eventually separated. The pressure of life, kids, me, everything, no one was to blame; it was just life. I miss my kids, and it's horrible, but I see them every other weekend and whenever I want. But I struggle, I really struggle. I don't think I'm a very good dad. I struggle with simple things like board games, playing cards, and going to the park. There is no denying the love I feel for both my children. They are truly amazing, and I am very proud of the way they are growing up; both are amazing kids. I've tried to reassure them that it is okay to talk. It's okay to talk about anything, no matter what happened, how bad you think it will be, or the trouble you may get into. We will always be here for you. They make me very happy, and guys, I love you so so much. I just don't think I'm a very good dad, and I'm truly sorry for that.

So that's me, now single and a part-time parent. It is not a pleasant feeling still. Vodka is cheap, and that will help. I wasn't really sure what I was looking for at the bottom of a bottle. I just wanted it all to end, the pain, the loneliness, my life.

This was no good, and nothing good would come from feeling like this, so the booze was tipped down the sink for the 100th time, and out came the dating apps.

I was on the internet dating scene for a while and had been chatting to a lovely woman who only lived a few miles away. We arranged to meet. I was sitting outside Starbucks waiting for her to arrive. When she appeared, she was pretty and much better looking than her pictures. I really need to get my eyes checked, though. I followed her up the stairs as you do, ladies first. Nice bum, nice figure. I had a latte, and she had a hot chocolate. We talked for hours and hours, and I couldn't get rid of her. She joined me for a trip around the local DIY Superstore. I had decided the garden needed a clematis in the attempt that one plant will make the six-foot fence disappear. I don't know much about plants, I'm afraid. We had to carry the conversation on in McDonalds as everywhere else was shut by now. As soon as I got home, I messaged her and told her how great it had been and how I would love to meet her again. She sent me a nipple pic.

We started to see each other more and more, and it was nice. We had a good connection together and had very similar interests. We both had two small children each. It was so nice to have them all together. It felt like I had the makings of a nice family unit. We decided it would be a good idea to move in together and save money, but also, we could spend more time together. Our lives seemed to be great. We both had good jobs and not a very big mortgage at all, with some lovely holidays abroad every year. I felt life was getting so much better.

We have a bit of a joke in our house that birthdays are always crap. Well, her 40th was no exception. I ended up being made redundant from my job and had to find something to bring in some money. So, I started working at a local hotel as the maintenance guy. The owner of the hotel had recently lost a friend to the dreaded C word and was attending her funeral. I felt sorry for him as the night porter was on annual leave. The owner had to work a night shift and then go to the funeral after staying up working all night. I couldn't have that, so I offered to stand in for him so he could say his goodbyes properly.

I started the night shift but wasn't feeling it. I was tired again, and my stomach was hurting, possibly something I had eaten. It was getting worse to the point, I thought, I'm going to need to call someone here. Never google your symptoms unless you're on the NHS website because before you know it, that small cut on your finger will turn into a brain tumour. Please don't do it. All the information you need is on the official NHS website. When it comes to Mental Health, then it's Mind. I called the 111 NHS line, and we talked about my symptoms. I explained I was looking after a hotel full of residents, so I couldn't leave, not until I got relieved in the morning. They decided the best action would be to send an out-of-hours doctor to my location to check in on me. I spent the next few hours lying on a sofa in the lounge area in pain. Making the odd trip to the communal toilets to throw up.

The doctor arrived, and we talked about what was going on. I should take some paracetamol and see my doctor in the morning. She would also give me a ring at about 7:00 am to check in on me just to make sure that I was okay. Luckily, one of the chefs had turned up to work a little early, so I left them in charge and headed home. I was just about to get into bed after explaining to the missus what was going on when the doctor called.

"With your history and everything going on, I have contacted the local hospital, and they are expecting you shortly."

I got the missus to drive. I was in pain, lots of pain.

We talked to another doctor, and I had observations done. They couldn't find anything wrong. So, I was sent to a ward for further tests. I was zoned out most of the time; something was not right, but they didn't know what it was. No raised temperature and blood levels were all satisfactory. My missus said it was the worst she had ever seen me, lying on the hospital bed looking grey, looking half dead. She says I looked like I was going to die. The doctor came to do his rounds and explained that nothing was showing up on any tests.

"We are not sure what's going on in your body, but we can see something is. The best thing to do would be to give you an operation. To see what's happening inside."

Great, another operation is just what I need right now. So, yet again, that was it. More risk assessments were completed, and I was put to sleep and back under the knife.

I woke up back in the ward, and the doctor was talking to my significant other.

"He had a burst appendix. It was the worst case of gangrene I have seen for a long time."

Thank God they decided to do an investigation. I was so relieved that after about a week, I was able to go home. It was my partner's 40th birthday coming up, and I had some making up to do.

It was only a swollen arm at first, but boy, did it hurt. The burning sensation, the heaviness of it, like you're dragging a log behind you.

"Happy 40th Birthday, my love".

I gave her the presents I had wrapped up from another hospital bed. I had been readmitted, another couple of weeks in hospital on a drip, another infection. Luckily, they put me in the private section. I had my own room and private toilet, and even a view over the countryside.

Chapter Six
Do you Know why you're here?

Mission Impossible was currently showing at the local cinema. I knew I shouldn't be going, but I just didn't want to break the news to her. I couldn't break the news to her. She would be devasted. But I had to. I just couldn't hide it anymore. My leg had started to swell up, and it was burning. I had a feeling; I knew what it was: another blood clot.

Well, that's exactly what it was, and to top it off, I had clots in my lungs, too. Pulmonary Embolism was not the greatest thing to have. More treatment, more time spent inside. The amount of blood tests I have had is crazy. X-rays scan the works. It's hard to knock the NHS. They have always been there for me.

I had to have a bone marrow sample taken. Wow, that was horrendous, especially when you're scared of needles. It felt like the doctor was putting a kebab skewer deep inside my spine till it hit the bone. Then WHACK, it felt like she had hit the damn thing with a hammer.

"Got to get through the bone somehow. Sorry"

She declared. Not long after, she started to panic a little about the amount of blood I was losing.

"Are you on any blood thinning medication?"

"Yes, I am, Rivaroxaban."

"That will explain it then, just keep sucking on the gas and air."

Sample taken, and with lots of tears and a tonne of gas and air, I had a follow-up appointment with the haematology doctor.

The doctor explained to me what had caused the Deep Vein Thrombosis and the Pulmonary Embolism. I had a condition called an

MPN. It's too long-winded to give you the technical name. Just google it if you're interested.

The type of MPN I have is called Polycythemia Vera, or PV for short. Obviously, the first question was.

"Is it cancer?"

"Well, it's a type of cancer, but you shouldn't be worried about the word cancer. The World Health Organisation likes to group things together, and as you have mutated blood cells, they have to class it as cancer. Any form of mutated cells is classed as cancer. Anyway, it's not cancer that will grow into a tumour".

It affects my blood; my body keeps producing blood clots, as far as I believe. I have a JAK-2 mutation. I'm an X-Man, a proper mutant now. More drugs are required.

Because the doctor had explained it was a blood cancer and not cancer that was going to spread and kill me within months or years, I was quite reassured. If I'm honest, it was more a case of, oh well, just more drugs to take. More crap, but whatever, laugh it off and crack on. Buried deep, just like all the other crap stuff in my life. I just kept saying.

"It's better that I have it than a little kid. The statistics say that about 2 people per 100,000 get this every year. So, I'm just glad I took a little kid's spot".

Medication came in the form of weekly injections that my wife had to give me at home. I didn't get on with the injections very well. Sometimes, I would cry whilst the missus was doing it, needles, and I don't really get on. The biggest thing for me was one of the side effects. Depression and the very low moods I would have, I just put it down to everything in my head that I have been battling to contain all the years. Anti-depressants wouldn't hurt. I've been on them plenty of times throughout my life. What's another pill every day?

I used to work in the maintenance industry doing property maintenance, fixing issues, and that type of stuff. No, it's not like you read in the books or watch on Confessions of a Window Cleaner. Not all the lonely housewives want to throw themselves at you. In a seven-year career, I've had it once.

I was attending a house because of a leak coming from a shower, a trace and assess job. The type of job you always click "NO" to when renewing your house insurance. A small, slim lady answered the door, dressed in a short satin black negligee. The shower was on the top floor of her newly built townhouse. The leak was coming from her ensuite. I kneeled down in front of the shower to remove the plinth and start my inspection. She kneeled down beside me. Legs open, all on show. I quickly turned my head and got on with my job, task firmly in hand. She took me downstairs to the middle floor as she wanted to show me the stains on the wall and ceiling from the leak. Then downstairs again, the same marks, in the same place. She told me the floor was wet and I should feel it, to check for myself. I knelt down and placed my palm on the floor. Yes, it was wet. She knelt down in front of me, ass in the air with nothing left to the imagination.

"Come feel how moist it is. Come over and feel it."

I quickly finished my inspection and retreated to my van.

I didn't have the best start in the property game. All my skills came from watching and helping my dad with DIY. I had no idea how to hang a door at the start, but I would consider myself quite a good chippy nowadays, even though some would probably disagree. I had to visit a rental property not long after I started taking blood thinners to control the blood clots. I was there to lay some flooring in the kitchen, which is not a favourite job of mine, but it pays the bills.

I got the roll of flooring out of the van and started to fit it nicely and neatly. I was trimming the edges with a new hooked blade in my Stanley knife when it slipped. Straight through my tough work trousers right into my thigh on my right leg. Blood started pouring out of me, and I knew as soon as I had done it that it wasn't going to be good. I rushed out to the van and pulled my trousers off. There I am, standing in the middle of a residential street, wearing a T-shirt complete with purple and white striped boxer shorts. There was quite a lot of blood, so I grabbed my first aid kit and applied some bandages over the wound, wrapping them extremely tight to stem the bleeding, then bound my leg up with some red electrical tape. Even John J Rambo would have been proud of me. The woman in the house asked if I was okay, and did. I needed an ambulance. She could see the amount of blood everywhere. But I went back to finishing her flooring, trying my best to keep my leg out straight. Job done. I just need to wash my trousers, as they are now covered and soaked in blood. I think I need to slow down a little and be a bit more careful.

One of the things that was making me quite stressed lately was Covid. It had been around now for a while, and I can still remember someone at work talking about Corona at the very start. It was in the news in China; I just laughed it off and brought a case of it on the way home.

"That won't come to anything."

How wrong was I!

I was due to fly out to New York with the missus on a short break. We had booked a trip a while ago, and as we were now engaged, she talked about getting married out there.

We flew out on an early February morning only to wait in an immigration hall for about 3 hours trying to get into the country. We were not worried about Corona then. It was only in China, only the odd death. It was a little concerning seeing all the flights coming in from China, though, all the people wearing surgical masks. Did they know something we didn't? Everyone was asking the question. There was not much else to talk about, standing there waiting.

The trip was amazing, it really was, and I have to say, although we were worried about the weather, you never know what you're going to get in February. It could be ten feet of snow. We arrived at our hotel just off Times Square and dropped our cases, then went off to have a wander. It was actually quite nice; we were walking around in T-shirts.

New York was an amazing place; we visited the Twin Towers Memorial, and that is just an amazing place. The tribute to all the fallen, it felt very special to be there and to pay our respects. A free trip on the Staten Island ferry to see the Statue of Liberty. Did you know it was given to the States by the French as a gift for the American Revolution in the 1880s? Chinatown didn't really do it for me. I was trying to put myself there as my connections to China. My home town my birthplace, although I'm not sure. Back in 1976, you could have picked up a genuine Rolex for a few dollars. We visited DUMBO, and if you go to New York, have a wander it's a great place. We walked over the Brooklyn Bridge and visited Wall Street. It was fantastic. We wanted to go up a skyscraper to view the city, but after the first day, the weather had turned, now mostly drizzle and low clouds. We didn't think it would be worth it. It's such a shame. The rooftop bar on 230 Fifth was excellent, with great views of the Empire State Building all lit up at night. Always carry ID in New York, and don't smoke or vape around ground zero.

We were due to get married on Wednesday, only two days time. We had to pick a location for the ceremony. All we had to do was let the wedding company know. We scouted out a few locations from DUMBO to Grand Central Station but decided it was going to be Ladies Pavilion, Central Park. It was such an amazing day. I wore a Navy suit, and she wore a lovely white wedding dress, so beautiful. Complete with Converse shoes, pink laces, and writing on the side. Her new surname on one foot and our wedding date on the other 05/02/2020, New York.

We had gotten a cab from our hotel to Central Park, where we were due to meet the wedding photographer and celebrant, Reid. It was quite a chilly day, and it didn't help we waited about 15 minutes for them to arrive. I'm always thinking that this guy has just scammed us out of our money. Are we just going to stand here like idiots until we realise? A woman walked up to us and, in a deep American accent, said.

"Oh my gosh, are you a bride?"

"Yes, I am".

Gleamed my soon-to-be new wife, hopefully.

Finally, my suspicion disappeared when I saw Goren walking towards us, smiling, carrying her flowers and my buttonhole. We had some pictures taken and then walked down to the little seating area called the Ladies Pavilion. We both said our I do's. It was a great feeling. More pictures, then we walked back to grab another cab as we had a very special place to visit. A church just a few blocks away, the very church her great-grandmother had got married in. She had arrived in New York on her own via boat in the early 1900s. She met a man and got married in the church we were now standing outside of. Later in life, she left to live in Luxemburg. It was a magical moment for my new wife and some memories she will never forget.

We had planned to spend the last day of the trip doing Central Park, starting at the top and working our way down. We were having such a lovely day and got as far as the Castle and the Ramble when I received a text message from our airline saying our flight home had been cancelled. We took a seat and tried to get hold of someone but to no avail. We had no option but to abandon our trip around Central Park and to get back to the hotel to log onto the internet and sort this out.

We should have been leaving for the airport at about 5:00 pm. However, we had to get an earlier flight, so that was it. Our time was done, and we had to make a dash for the airport and catch a flight. A massive storm was closing in, and planes might have to be grounded. Definitely no visits to the cockpit in this day and age. It's so sad. I loved driving the plane as a kid. As it turns out, it wasn't too bad. We got a new flight, and the tailwind was so strong we went from New York JFK to London Heathrow in under five hours, Four hours, and 57 minutes. In fact, Virgin Atlantic Flight number 4. I believe at some points in the journey, we were travelling over 820mph. The pilot was so excited when we landed; we had just broken the crossing record. Only to be dashed as the plane that did the same route ten minutes before us beat us by a few seconds.

The absolute number 1 thing to do in New York. Grab a slice of pie that's pizza to the rest of us from the cheap little restaurants and side stalls. You can get a plain Margarita pizza, a massive slice, for $1. We couldn't resist them so nice. Eat them the correct way, too, and fold them in half.

Back to normal life again and back to Covid. The first lockdown was great. The sun was out, and I was shielding at home as a result of my weakened immune system. I sat in the garden most days, drinking Corona away one bottle at a time, topping up my tan on furlough. The second lockdown was not so great. I was pretty much banned from going out of the house. My wife was paranoid I would get it and die. At the end of the day, that's what we were all being told. Especially with my health issues, I have to SHIELD.

Staying at home is fine, but not when it's cold and you can't go out. I had just had an eye test and was deciding on what style of glasses I wanted, but because of Covid, I just gave up and got a set from the Pound Shop. It's not as if I was going to be able to get out and visit some castles or anything anytime soon.

Even though I'm scared of needles, I couldn't wait to get jabbed this time. I even cried with relief when that first dose went into my arm. Although, yes, I do worry the jab hasn't been long-term tested, and we don't know if anything will come up in years to come, but I'm just happy to be alive. I can see it now in all the adverts on the TV.

"Did you have the COVID jab?

Get in touch now. You could be entitled to compensation."

I was glad I got my jabs early, and although deeper depression was setting in, I was able to leave the house to go and grab some shopping, even if it was only click-and-collect. So, there you go, more pills, more health issues, more crap to deal with. Just don't think about it, file it away, laugh it off, man up, and get on with it.

They say your head is like a filing cabinet, but I like to put a modern-day twist on it. To me, your brain is like a smartphone. It takes pictures and saves videos. It takes notes and stores all the information and files it away in its correct place. The more information you take in, the more data it stores, but like anything, it's got a limit to the amount of data it can handle. It's got a memory, and that can only take so much. Some people's memory may be better and capable of storing more information, and some have better processing speeds. There are different types on the market. You can delete information, but it's always there in the background somewhere. Come on, you don't actually know what the Cloud is, do you and the fact everything we say and do is recorded. How many times have you been chatting to someone about something?

"I think we should get a new kettle. Ours doesn't seem to be heating up correctly".

I guarantee you the next day. Your media is going to be full of kettles for sale or Curry's adverts. You can clean your files and keep them in order, maybe do system updates from time to time, and Download more Apps for more information. The downside to all this memory is that it can't take anymore, can't process anymore. Shut down, SHUT DOWN.

That's what happened to me. My head could not take any more of anything. It exploded at that time, at that place, gone. I had no control over it.

It just exploded like a nuclear bomb, BOOM!

View of the Empire State Building from the Roof Top Bar at 230 & 5th.

Thank you, Here B Barr, for all the travel advice. I cannot wait to return.

New York is a fascinating place to visit. This picture is taken at DUMBO. Down Under the Manhattan Bridge Overpass.

I can't wait to go back and tour Central Park, properly this time!

Chapter Seven
The Gargoyle Returns

It was Monday, 22nd August 2022, and we had just returned from a family holiday abroad to visit my parents in Cyprus. It was a great break full of sunshine and beaches. The kids loved it, spending time in the waterpark whilst we relaxed on a kabana soaking up the Mediterranean summer sun. Swimming with the sea turtles and jumping off the top deck of the boats. It was especially nice to see mum and dad again; it's been far too long, and I really miss you both. I was getting lots of text messages from one of my work colleagues all about issues that were going on back at work, a holiday of stress and wondering what was going on and what I was going to come back to.

Monday morning came around, and back to work, I went. I spoke to my boss in the morning and told him I couldn't cope anymore and how stressed I was. We had a chat, and after a while, I went back to my desk. I don't know why or what made me do it, but I opened up my phone and clicked the Safari icon. Into the search field, I typed Alwyn Clayton Cirencester. A few articles filled the screen.

"Man 62, jailed after admitting indecent assault on teenager."

I opened it up and read the article. It was him; it was Alwyn. I just sat there in shock. What do I do, how do I handle this, what happens now?

The reality is for quite a while now, I haven't been coping. I knew I was stressed out and quite bad, too. Seeing that article made my head explode. I walked into my boss's office, sat down, and showed him the article.

"He did it to me!"

We sat, and we talked, and then I went back to my work. My boss read the other articles about him and found out he had passed away. My mind is just doing cartwheels. What do I do now? I took a walk and called 101. I spoke to the police and told them my story. The guy on the other end was so nice and so compassionate. He listened to all the details. An awful lot of details, I spilt my guts, there and then down the phone to some stranger. Hundreds of times worse than Chunk ever did!

I knew I would have to go home and tell the wife. I can't do it; I can't break this news to her. What have I done?

My wife has always thought something was not quite right with me. I have two places on my body that I can't be touched, on my side by my waist. The faintest of touches just send ripples of pain and hurt through my whole body. I get a sudden image in my head of him kneeling down In front of me in the woods. Unzipping my trousers, both hands holding onto my waist. It repulses me, and I hate being touched on those spots. My wife does ask me why I flinch and go weird when she occasionally touches me there, mainly by accident.

"It's where I had my operation. Always feels weird there, don't know why, sorry."

She never pushed it; she thought it was because of my grandad!

We do some crazy thinking when the head goes. Everything just happens. It's like you have no control over what's going on around you at that point. When I got home from work, I acted normal. We talked in the kitchen about normal things, and then I took her upstairs. We laid on the bed together, and I held her hand. I told her what had happened, and then I cried. We both cried. She asked me how it all happened, and for some reason, I thought it would be a good idea to film it. Me talking about my story for the very first time after all these years. I set the phone up and hit record. I told my wife my story and didn't leave anything out. I needed this recording for the future. Already I was thinking how I've been a total idiot all my life, why haven't I shouted about this sooner? Why have I had to wait for 30-odd years?

You need to speak!

I needed to get it on film and release it to the world, to shout it from the rooftops. I wanted everyone to know. I contacted the Sun, the Daily Mail, and all the local outlets to tell my story, but no one ever replied, and I don't know why. I still can't be believed.

My wife was so supportive, shocked, and in a state of confusion but so, so supportive. We talked until the early hours before the sleeping pills took effect. We both had headaches from all the tears. It's not been an easy thing for me to talk about. It's been inside me, hiding for over thirty years. I went to work the next morning but couldn't concentrate on anything. My head was a scrambled mess. A kaleidoscope affect, my head just spinning. That was the last day I worked, and have not been back since. I can't face the world right now.

I received a phone call from a company called First Light and started speaking with Rachel. She would be someone to talk to whilst help was sorted for me. I was in a total state of shock. Finally, I had spoken about what had happened, and it felt good to release it after all these years. It felt good to have the support of my wife, but life got tough very quickly.

The days spent In bed, not being able to move. Playing a game of head, shoulders, knees and toes just to get the leg to do a little twitch to start the movement and hope the momentum would get me out of my pit. I had to tell my parents what had all happened via WhatsApp. Horrendous when all you want is a cuddle and someone to say.

"It's gonna be alright".

Knowing all the time that they are going to blame themselves for all of this. We sat my step kids down and told them what had happened and what was now going on. My kids are not daft. They know something's wrong with Daddy, but they don't know the full story. They are too young to handle that at the moment.

Yes, it's hard, and yes, it's stressful, but I would do it again in a heartbeat. Why had I waited all these years? The Shame and the guilt, the fear no one would believe me, that's why.

But they did. They all believed me. The one thing I have wanted all these years is for someone to believe my story. Seeing him in the paper and knowing he had been convicted for doing the same thing to someone else. With very similar stories, I knew people would believe me now. I knew it was my time, and I don't regret it, not one bit.

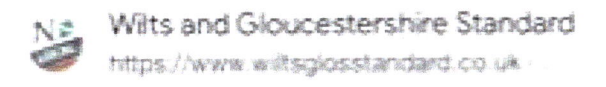

Wilts and Gloucestershire Standard
https://www.wiltsglosstandard.co.uk

Man, 62, jailed after admitting indecent assault on teenager

1 Feb 2010 — Alwyn Clayton, 62, from Cirencester, pleaded guilty at Gloucester Crown Court on December 18 to two counts of indecent assault against a ...

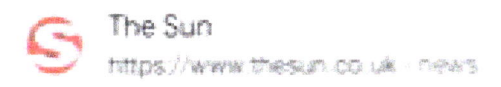

The Sun
https://www.thesun.co.uk › news

Polo club worker was abused by paedophile bar boss while Prince ...

4 Aug 2018 — The victim was just 14 when Alwyn Clayton started grooming him with cash and plying him with drink and drugs. Advertisement. Prince Charles ...

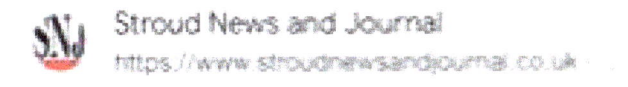

Stroud News and Journal
https://www.stroudnewsandjournal.co.uk

Police Investigation Results In Man Being Sentenced To Three Years For Indecent ...

29 Jan 2010 — 62-year-old Alwyn Clayton pleaded guilty at

This is the page that came up, the page when I googled him

I just wish I had seen it sooner.

Chapter Eight
The Brick Walls

Help is there, and people want to help, most of them anyway. Like I said, it's not going to be easy. I've had so many brick walls thrown up around me along the way. Just when you think things are going okay, something happens that gets you so enraged it hurts.

The first hurdle I came across was getting help. I had started to feel very, very low when I came out about my abuse. The emotions just flood in. Moving, sleeping, and concentrating on normal daily life gets hard. In fact, it got really hard, really quick. You can stay in bed all day long, not being able to move. Physically not able to move, it's a strange feeling. You cry at the drop of a hat; you wake up crying, and it can continue for hours and hours Until the tears run out. There are times when I really need to cry, but I just can't.

That's when the headaches start from all the crying. If it's safe to do, then please keep some aspirin or similar for the headaches and a glass of water by your bed. A large bottle is better. Challenge yourself to drink it all in a day.

Panic attacks can come on at any moment, the tightening of the chest. The breathing changes, rapid, short, then long and drawn out. Try to relax. I know that's not easy, but think of a happy place.

The twitches are the worst. My arms and legs just tense up all the time, tensing every muscle in my body constantly. I'm not even in control of it. I can be talking to you one minute, then wallop the arms just start going. It happens all the time, and an episode can last a few seconds to hours. I've even given every movement a name. Rexy is when I pull my arms up and tense them over and over. It's like I'm doing an impression of a T-Rex with my little curled-up arms in front of me. I call the chicken wings Ginger from Chicken Run. Just pretend you're a small bird flapping your wings, trying to fly. Rexy, Ginger and the gang really do help me sometimes.

Disassociation is the feeling you get when you're viewing what's happening from a distance. It's almost like you're watching yourself from a few inches behind your body. Just looking down at yourself, feeling not connected. The feeling that everything happens in slow motion and is not real in some way.

The constant jaw ache from clenching your teeth over and over. The ringing in the ears going up, now at full volume level 10. It's hard, it's really hard. You might get one of these things, or you might get them all, maybe even more. Everyone is different. This is just what happens to me. I'm not going to sugarcoat it; you think you're going to die; I've had panic attacks so bad strangers have had to call me an ambulance. I honestly thought I was going to die. It's not a nice feeling! My wife said I should carry a paper bag around with me just in case I have a panic attack whilst I'm out. The reality is I don't need a paper bag to breathe into. My panic attacks don't work like that. My attacks feel like my whole body is failing in some way. Your entire body draining of life and existence. All collapsing in on itself, you can almost see and feel a light at the end of the tunnel wanting to draw you in. If you're lucky, you might skip the paranoia. I'm so scared all the time. I tip-toe around the house at night like a burglar from a cartoon, complete with a swag bag and dressed in a black and white striped jumper, almost like the Hamburglar, shaking like a leaf. Constantly looking for him, hiding in the corners, just waiting for him to pounce.

My wife was downstairs making a cup of tea one morning. I needed the toilet, so I had to drag myself out of my bed. Climbing out of bed, I felt like I was abseiling down a mountain on SAS Who Dares Wins. I'm probably making the noises, too, the grunts and the groans as I'm moving my body around. The wife comes through the bedroom door, and half a second later, the smell hits us both. She literally scared the shit out of me. The only saving grace was the dog was on the bed and not in his basket! I guess every cloud has a silver lining. I believe it's pretty normal to be hypervirulent in cases like these.

That wasn't the worst one, though. I have to try and plan my days around how I feel and what I'm capable of completing in a day. On this particular day, I needed to head into the town centre. I like going around charity shops and finding objects that stand out to me, curiosities and the like, anything random. I have quite a collection now. It's a way of getting out of the house and trying to meet new people. The wife goes mad at some of the crap I buy, but it's a way of keeping me grounded. I've also started to collect some of my old toys, the toys I used to play with as a child. Unfortunately, most of them were left behind when we moved back to the UK from America. My toy dinosaurs and toy soldiers, all my old Star Wars toys, things I can look at and touch. Things I can play with when I'm feeling down. Items I can look up the history of and wonder. Let my mind drift off to the olden days, what life was like back then. These will be my ground anchors, my safe room where, no matter what happens, I can go to and play. I can look at the walls and touch things, then drift away and try to relax.

I was walking around the town centre in the rain with my winter coat on. An old man was busking. He was like one of these one-man bands. He was great at singing country and western songs.

"Country roads take me home to a place I belong."

It's by John Denver and is one of my favourites. It reminds me of a happy place, my childhood in the US. I listened to a few songs and dropped a few pound coins into his guitar case, then walked away. I'm not sure what happened, but some youths started running, heading towards me. One of them shouted something, but I'm not sure what it was or if it was directed at me or not. That's when I could feel it coming out of me. I do hope diarrhoea is not hereditary. I hear it runs in the genes! So, on a wet winter's day, I am the only one walking through the town centre in a polo shirt with my coat wrapped around my waist, desperately trying to hide the stains seeping through my jeans. On the odd occasion, I have even resorted to wearing those nappie pants for men, just in case.

Anyway, back to the book. I was talking to Rachel from First Light; they were trying to find counselling services that could help me. I was recommended a few, but I kept getting told it could be months and months to wait, and they all work on a self-referral basis. Luckily, First Light would be in contact every week, and I could contact Rachel if I needed to. It was nice to talk to Rachel every week, and it did not matter what about. It was just nice to have someone there who wanted to help.

The local policing team had realised there was a gap in the service, and that's where First Light came in. I believe they work alongside the SARC's unit. It really was amazing to finally be able to talk to someone. Someone who would listen to you, no matter what you talked about. No judgment, no preconceived ideas or thoughts about you. I was so very grateful to Rachel and the team; they would be offering me support until I got into a service that could help. This is something that needs to be set up nationwide! I often wonder what way my life would have gone if I didn't have Rachel to talk to. Thank you Rachel.

It really does knock you when you know it could be months to wait for help. I need the help now. That's not the fault of Rachel or the team. It's a fact that there are too many people out there suffering already and nowhere near enough help. I'm currently on a waiting list for a specialist charity that deals with people with issues similar to mine. I believe they have 140 full-time counsellors. There is currently a waiting list of 12 to 18 months. Sadly, they are not taking on any new referrals at the moment, to be reviewed in six months' time.

Yes, this sounds totally shit, and that's because it is. Please don't let that put you off though. No matter how hard it gets, just remember you have survived 100% of your bad days so far. Too many people need help, and there is nowhere near enough help available.

We were so fortunate that we were in a position to pay for the counselling I needed and start to try and make sense of what was going on in my head. That's why Rachel introduced me to a charity called IPSUM.

IPSUM is based in Swindon. I was referred to them and started counselling sessions within about three months, and that's quick by all accounts.

I was also waiting for the police to contact me about making a proper statement about what had happened all those years ago, but because the perpetrator had passed away, they did not see any rush to get this done. It was a very long, agonising, frustrating time. All I wanted to do was talk to them and tell them what had happened. If I'm honest, I just felt because it was historic and he was dead that, they just didn't care.

I did have an email from them a few months later to say I could come into the police station. Finally, I got my opportunity to speak. I couldn't wait to talk to them after all these years. It was the day before I was due to attend the cop shop when I had a call from the PC that was assigned to my case. As I had given quite a lot of details about what had already happened previously, they had the basics of the story. I was told that as the perpetrator has passed away, they would not be in a position to open an investigation, and although they would be happy to hear what I had to say, they could not and would not open any investigations. If I wanted to come in and talk, I could, but in reality, it would be pointless. I didn't bother. What was the point? They weren't going to do anything they don't care. I felt so let down, so badly let down. If he was Jimmy Saville, I'm sure they would be interested. The system is so wrong. I get it; I really do. You can't prosecute a dead person. They just don't have the resources to deal with it. I let it beat me up for a few weeks, and then I contacted them again. I had to tell my story; it needed to be heard. So, we made another appointment. I was walking down the street, tightly holding onto my wife's hand. I opened the door, and we walked into the foyer of the police station. We got to the reception and booked in, then waited for the PC to turn up. We got put in a side room and just had a chat about it all. What happened, how and when, all the info, lots of info. She took a few notes and said she would pass some details on to the CID team, as I have mentioned quite a lot that they might need to look into. I wondered if my dad's mate would hear about it all.

I have to say I felt disgusted at the way it was handled, not by the PC but by the system. She was full of empathy, and I'm not saying that in a sarcastic way. I've seen dramas on TV and programmes like 24 Hours in police custody. I had an idea what to expect when I turned up at the police station. They would take me into a quiet room, and it would all be video recorded as evidence. I felt like I needed to be treated like any other victim of a serious sexual assault. To me, it didn't matter it was 30 years ago. I'm reliving it now. Here and now, today, this minute, this very second. It's happening, it is real, it is real to me. I needed to be treated like a rape victim would have been treated, instead just a side room with a notebook. People were talking on the other side of the door in the reception area. I think someone was talking about a lost dog! If I'm honest, I didn't feel very comfortable speaking just in case people on the other side of the door could hear me.

I have been given quite a bit of help from the doctors, but again, that's not easy. I went to the doctor with my wife at the very start. I spilt my guts again. It all came out the whole lot. The doctor was shocked at everything I was saying and said I may have PTSD. I talked about First Light and Rachel and how they were going to help me. So, as far as they were concerned, I was getting help and kept taking the pills. I called the doctor's surgery one day for an appointment. You have to call at 8 am for a same-day appointment. In reality, it's constantly engaged and can take an hour to get to talk to someone. I spoke to the lady on reception, who was clearly having a good morning! I told her I was feeling low and needed to see a doctor to get some medication sorted anything.

"Sorry, no appointment left today. Phone back tomorrow".

I told her I was thinking of throwing myself in front of a train.

"Sorry, we don't have an appointment today; you will have to call back tomorrow".

Really, come on!

If we didn't have enough to deal with, my wife found a lump on her breast a few months back. She doesn't like leaving me on my own, so I went with her to the doctor to get it looked at. I kept telling my wife it was probably nothing and to try not to worry. I was bricking it. I was convinced she had breast cancer and was going to die. I had a full-on panic attack in front of the doctor. My wife explained to her what was going on. The doctor looked at me sobbing, and all cured up in the chair, then she looked at my wife.

"We are not here today to talk about his problems but to look at your lump".

I was told to go and wait in the car by the doctor, as she had other people to see. I had to walk past all the other people in the reception area, crying my eyes out and having a full-on panic attack. It wasn't a nice feeling.

My wife was sent to the hospital for some tests, and to be fair, they were amazing. They soon came to the conclusion that it was a cyst, and it was drained out there and then, and no one could knock the efficiency of that.

We were quite lucky that my wife told me I needed to take out an insurance policy for income protection. My job didn't pay sick pay, so we needed it. We had just moved to a much bigger house on the edge of the town, so she wanted the protection, just in case anything happened. I contacted the insurance company and gave them the details of my illness. They sent me a claim form. There was a section that needed to be filled out by the doctors, dates and diagnoses that type of thing.

I eventually received an email from my insurance company. We are not paying out on your claim. The doctors had not ticked a box to say I have been diagnosed by a therapist, with many letters behind their name! This meant I did not fit their criteria, so I called them up for a little chat.

"Really, the doctors have diagnosed me with PTSD, Panic attacks and anxiety, and you're saying that's not good enough. It's the doctors, the NHS, for God's sake. How much higher can you go!"

I had a full-on meltdown on the phone with them. I feel so sorry for the guy on the other end listening to me ranting. At one point, I said.

"Because you have stressed me out so much with all this. You make it so hard to claim. I am going to pour petrol on myself and set myself on fire".

I was close to jumping out of my third-floor bedroom window at that very moment.

"I'm going to make a stand in front of your office. I'm going to martyr myself and walk into the foyer covered in flames."

My wife didn't really like hearing this, so the Community Mental Health team got involved, AWP.

I had a quick chat with Avon and Wiltshire Partnership on the phone, an assessment asking me different questions on everything. How I am feeling, what my eating habits are like. Do I wash and shower, that type of thing? They have come back with a diagnosis of Complex PTSD; they also don't think therapy will help me at this stage. They are not sure if I'm ready for any treatment as I also have disassociation. But as I am currently seeing IPSUM, they are happy for me to keep going with this if I think it's helping me.

It is by the way, it's difficult and I feel so sorry for Cerian, my counsellor. She makes it easier to deal with and in a way that I can understand and comprehend. So that was it me, all wrapped up in a simple phone conversation and a letter. The only good thing that came out about the Community Mental Health Team getting involved was, they sorted out what was required by the insurance company. They have started paying my claim out, it's not much but it helps. On the down side I can't help but think well is that it, you're the NHS Mental Health team you have diagnosed me with Complex PTSD and, carry on as you are, even though you think it's not right for me. I was expecting an action plan anything. This is what we can do for you, this is what the plans are. On this day you need to see this person. On this date this is going to happen, but nothing. Do give us a bell anytime, if you need to talk. Where is my recovery plan? I need your help, you're the NHS for crying out loud, please help me! I so wish Mental Health problems presented themselves as a lump!

It can get so very stressful; it feels like everything you do; these walls just get thrown up around you. People always say we are here to help. When it comes to it, I feel most people are just like a consultation service. Oh, this is how you feel, let me send you some links of charity's that can help you with that. But you will have to refer yourself to anything and if you can afford to pay for it then great otherwise you could be waiting a very long time. Trust me I have enough to deal with at the moment without having to find my own answers. That's why I'm asking for the help from the National Health Service, I don't know where to start.

Rachel helped me so much at the start getting me into IPSUM and I will never forget the chats we used to have. Thank you, Rachel, I wish you peace and happiness.

Talking to Cerian has been truly amazing, I have never met someone so passionate about how good life can be than her. The NHS doesn't think that's right for me though. Then tell me what is please!

I went for another doctor's appointment as I have been having terrible diarrhoea at the moment, also we can't keep buying carpet cleaner! I have convinced myself that I have prostate cancer. So off I went and spoke to the doctor, again. I told him what was going on and my thoughts. I need to give a stool sample. I'm not really sure how I'm going to get runny diarrhoea in a small bottle but Doc suggested I crap in an ice cream tub and scoop it out. He asked if everything else was ok.

"I'm concerned and getting worried that I am becoming a paranoid schizophrenic with a multiple personality disorder".

He just stared at me for a moment.

"What would you like me to do with that information?"

"Help me!"

He looked through my notes and, as I had been given, the text links to Mind and Lift Psychology. I tried to tell him these places were not right for me, he simply replied.

"Well, that's all the help we can offer!"

I think I need to have a conversation with my counsellor tonight see what she thinks and go from there. Keep taking the pills and standing guard at my window.

About a month later AWP did get in touch with me, we had a five-minute conversation over the phone. They have reassured me I'm not a paranoid schizophrenia and don't have a multiple personality disorder. So, I'm glad that was all sorted out.

I have also started to become a service user of the Kelly Foundation Swindon; they are trying to build up my courage around other people. All whilst doing something I enjoy. Welcome to Camera Club!

The car was parked and I walked along the foot path towards the entrance, It's the first time I have been here and the place looks like a smaller version of a Travel Lodge. I wonder about all the people inside their rooms, people deemed not safe enough for society or themselves, wondering what Jack Nicholson would make of it all, or if anything has changed since his day. Hoping that one day I don't need that kind of help, hoping one day I don't have to turn up to that entrance, in crisis. I rang the bell as it was after hours and that's what the sign had told me to do. I waited and waited, then waited some more, even longer in fact. I gave up after that, but just before I went home I staired at the sign again. It was a sign that told me I should set up my own business. Auditing the Mental Health Services from an insider's point of view.

The sign that night simply read.

"For help ring bell"

Release that inner child. Get down on the floor and have fun.

My memory wall behind me. Full of anything and everything from my childhood.

*My wife hates it! I love it, these are my Ground Anchor**s**.*

How many things can you recognise?

Chapter Nine
The Diary Entry

Friday, 13th March 2023, and a bit of Saturday

First of all, sorry for the way this is written. I'm literally typing it all as it's playing out in my head. I thought it would be a good idea to write a diary of my day, a bit like Adrian Mole used to do. See if you can get a little sneak peek of what my days can be like and the things that go through my head.

I've just looked at my Echo device, and it's Friday 13th March. I already know the year, I think!

I woke up this morning with a headache. I'm not sure I'm drinking enough; my urine looks like orange juice and smells like sugar puffs. I'm ok. I had a shower a few days ago. A nice cuppa tea and a catch-up on the outside world, social media first, then the news all on my phone. Doom scrolling for hours. Come on, who doesn't like to watch videos of kittens and things you enjoy. I have to force myself to put the phone down.

Kate looks amazing as always and a nice touch. It's green for St Patrick's Day. It's Gold Cup Day, too. I'm tired, so my wife tells me to sleep, and to be honest, it feels like a good idea. I've set an alarm for an hour and a half's time. I cuddle the dog and drift off almost instantly.

10:30 comes, and I'm up and about, standing at my window and seeing what's happening. A wren keeps flying in and out at speed. It's probably the same one that I've been trying to photograph for the last few days. I throw the clothes on that I have been wearing all week, including the undercrackers. I can't see any visible skid marks, so they will do for another day or two. A little stain on my trousers, so I have to scrape some debris off. I'm not too worried about the stains on my hoodie. It's only golden syrup. I grab Scooby and take him around the block.

We only saw one old boy walking a golden retriever, and we said hello to each other. The dogs wanted to sniff each other's butts, so me and the old bloke are standing there, having the standard conversation on how dogs are weird.

"It's a good job humans don't greet each other the same way."

He went one way, and I went the other. One of the neighbours is having the windows replaced, and there are workmen outside his house talking. I position the dog between us and try to walk past as quietly as possible. I am quite tense. My teeth are gritted, arms locked tight into my side. It looks like Rexy and Ginger have come along for the walk, too. I dream that Scooby is a killer guard dog who will protect me if needed, the reality being he would lick you to death. It's a good job. It's only a few yards to my front door and safety.

I've had a plan to cook my wife a nice dinner. I have to pop to the chemist and grab some medication so I can pop into Asda.

Shopping wasn't great. Every aisle feels like a never-ending tunnel that I have to walk down. Everyone is staring at me; people are getting too close. I grab what I need and get out as quickly as I can.

The shopping has been put away, so I'm going to try my hand at flapjacks. I made some last week, and they were quite nice. I wonder where the dog is, so I trundle up the stairs. I'm totally out of breath before even getting up the final few, but it's all worth it. I'm greeted with a massive tail wag as always, so I join the little teddy bear on the bed. Scooby just wants kisses.

We settle down together and then begin to watch The Apprentice from catch up. It's the interviews this week, and I like this part.

I can hear people shouting outside, so I jump up to investigate. It is over the road, about 100 yards away. I decide to get my camera out as there are quite a lot of blue tits flying around. I captured some nice pictures of a female black cap. The shouting has stopped now, so I go back to the TV, back to The Apprentice. I have mixed feelings about The Apprentice as it's triggered me off before. I like Sir Alan Sugar and love my computer, the Amstrad CPC 464. I have so many memories of playing on the computer. Not all nice, unfortunately, but that's not Sir Alan's fault. It's a tough week with everything going on.

Cheltenham races are on, so I'm having lots of flashbacks, Images in my head, and feelings where I physically shake. I'm tense and hyper-vigilant. I dropped a tea bag on the floor this morning. My wife asked me if I had an accident on my way to the toilet. It's happened quite a lot over the last few months. I must clean that up. I've done a half-arse effort.

"Alexa, add Carpet Cleaner to the shopping list."

I went to the doctors the other day and told them I think I have paranoid schizophrenia with multiple personality disorder. I do have an irrational fear of people. Everyone always lets me down in some way or another. Whether it's been friends I've had in the past or people who have abused me, anyone and everyone hates me and wants to kill me. I'm not very good at the moment when I get upset. My flight kicks in, and I stand at the window, weighing up the options. If I jump, will it kill me or just bloody hurt? With my blood disorder, I would bleed out in a few minutes. So, the job would be done. But I don't want to bleed out and go in pain. Train it is, that's the best way, should be instant.

The poor train driver and it might not be as instant as I think. No, I'm going to jump off the multi-story carpark.

I have sent an email to the local Mental Health team telling them my concerns and asking for help, but I'm still waiting for a response. My counsellor called, and they can't make the appointment later, so I can't even talk to her about how I'm feeling. God, I feel so alone right now. I have been referred to a specialist counselling service, but it's a 12-month wait at the moment, and they have sent me an email to say they are not taking on any more referrals at the moment. I've also sent an email to my local councillor, MP, to discuss the failings in the services at the moment and what can be done. I've come up with a few ideas that could really help and really make a difference.

I feel like Humpty Dumpty right now.

"Humpty Dumpty sat on a wall. Humpty Dumpty had a great fall. All the king's horses and all the king's men couldn't put humpy together again!"

I hate horse racing, and every time I see a horse, it brings on flashbacks. Every time you walk past a betting shop, they are hard to ignore. They are everywhere now; the high street is full of them. We must start a campaign to bring back Woolworths. Time's getting on, so I need to cook dinner. Cauliflower steak for the wife, I'm not really that hungry.

The outside camera has gone off a few times, but it's just the neighbours and my stepson coming home, but you never know, so I always have to keep an eye out.

I have just been standing guard at my window, scanning like the Terminator or Robocop. I'm starting to think I actually do have a superpower.

I'm a real-life X-man. They are all mutants, well, so am I. All my blood cells have a mutation Jak 2 something. Therefore, my belief is I'm an X-man, a mutant, although I'm not sure what my name would be or my superpower. Now, do you see why I told the doctor my thoughts? I'm going to go now as I'm starting to get really tense. The legs, the chicken wings, and the T-Rex claws are back. Ears at level six. To top it all off, the dogs just farted, he had cauliflower earlier too.

You don't know what people are going through in their own lives, so it's best to be nice. The ringing has gone down to level four. I have the odd twitch, but it's mainly a little chicken.

My wife is getting a little annoyed with me for being on my phone again, tap tap tapping away. But when I have something in my head, I have to get it out, good or bad. Anyway, just because I'm not going to type it doesn't mean it's not going to be thinking it all night. So it's best to write it down somewhere and forget about it tonight. Put a pin in it.

I have been thinking about writing a chapter titled,

"What it's like living with Complex PTSD and being an Over Thinker."

The first line would simply say.

"Absolutely fucking draining. It's shit"

I've been keeping guard at my window and telling my wife about writing my diary entry, and I've told her what it consisted of and why I'm writing a book. It's simply because I want people to know what a day in my life feels like, all day and every day. It doesn't stop.

It's time to sleep as it's getting late, so I wish you a good night; I'm going to take some Zopiclone. The doctors have prescribed it for me. I try not to take them too often.

Sometimes, when I can't sleep, it's a good idea to do something else. Go into another room and read a book or something like that, only for half an hour. Stand up doing it so you don't get too comfy and end up there all night. Just half an hour, then go back to bed. Hopefully, drop off for a few hours rest. I know I'm going to think and dream about the races that happen every night. I've been dreaming and thinking about it a lot this week.

It's time to say hello to Ginger. That's what I call the tense arm thing, the chicken wings. The mermaid, that's the leg thing. Both legs tensing up and flapping around.

Pretend you're swimming like a mermaid, both legs together, and really tense your calf muscles.

FASTING, that's the stroke face. I call it this just because they say you need to act FAST when someone is having a Stroke. My face feels numb and droopy right now. The ringing in my ears is at level seven.

"Alexa, play thunderstorm sounds."

I try to imagine, with the help of the thunderstorm sounds, that the ringing in my ears is now part of a rain forest; the buzzing are the insects in the background.

Imagine you're a Fasting Ginger Mermaid who's listening to thunderstorm sounds. Throw in some Rexy, all whilst reliving what happened to you at the races. It's time to think of some happy thoughts. I love the Otters. They're cool; I hope it's nice tomorrow. I'm going to try and find them. I managed to film them feeding a while ago. No more negative thoughts tonight, please.

His friend is standing in the corner by the light, keeping an eye on me. Someone has just come into the room with us. He is behind me. The green and white striped waistcoat and bow tie. I'm not wearing any trousers. I'm woken up. We are driving down a country road. I'm sitting in the passenger seat, and it's really late; no one is around.

"That's where another of my friends got naked and was dancing around in the middle of the road a few years ago. He was so wasted!"

That's about all I can remember about the Gold Cup. That evening, the cocktails, the room, the people. Happy punters were throwing money at me. They were ever so nice. I can buy a new fishing rod now. Working at the racecourse was great. It didn't even feel like I actually did any work!

I loved playing Dungeons and Dragons, the Red Gargoyle.

I can see the house, and I can describe the layout. The L-shaped lounge, the open stairs, and the chimney breast. The dining table and almost matching sideboard, the open plan kitchen with a sticky out bit. Standing next to the worktop is the fridge freezer. The kitchen door leads out to some sort of lean-to. The garage door is on the left. That's where he kept the drugs, inside on top of the door lintel.

"I'm glad you came round. I've just got some new weed. Let's try it. Vodka and coke?"

"Yes, please."

"I've spoken to the lady on night shift, and she's up for it. I've got some new videos for us to watch."

I'm very open with my wife. We can talk about anything. She did throw me through one day, but I knew the question would come at some point.

"Did you cum?".

Well, the answer is yes, yes, I did because that's what happens when sexual things are happening to you and you think it's entirely normal. There is a thing called Stockholm Syndrome. It's a coping mechanism for a captive and abusive situation. We develop positive feelings towards our captors and abusers over time. You grow a bond an immensely deep bond. Trauma bonding, they call it now, days I don't know if I want to go and piss on his grave. I know some people do and crack on. If that's what you need, then do it. Just remember, it is probably illegal. For me, it wasn't the right thing to do. He would have enjoyed it too much. I want to skin him alive, rip every single piece of flesh off of his body. The next one is wanting him to hold me close and tell me he is sorry. I think Cerian and counselling are helping. I used to be so bad. Even with this, my wife still would have loved to have had a child with me. God, is she crazy?

She knows what she wants to be called when a grandkid comes along one day, but not too soon!

"I'm going to be called Nanny Ju Ju. What are you going to be called, Granddad?"

I used to go on holidays with my grandad. We would go to Hastings, where he had a caravan. It was amazing; he would spend all day and night in the club's bar, and I would walk around the lake. Go over the hills and down to the seafront. Then, I spent every evening with my friend Elliot. He was just as mad as me. We would have competitions to see who could jump the furthest and swing the highest. I can't tell you if my Grandad ever did anything to me. I hope I was one of the lucky grandkids. Yes, I remember being in the greenhouse, but nothing more than that.

"Grumpy, that's what I'm going to be called, but it won't be living in this house!"

I think I'm connecting with my inner child, my feelings at the time, and how I have dealt with it all; it's all my fault! Am I to blame?

I've been told I didn't have any control over what was happening and that I didn't have the skill to deal with it as a child. He wasn't my friend. He was my abuser.

When I'm very down and upset, I look at pictures of my kids, my wife, and my family. Birds and fishing, I try to remember nice things I have done in my life. I don't have a very good track record of horses, though. The first one I rode was on a mountain trail in the Rocky Mountains. It bolted and tried to throw me off a cliff. Luckily, the guide managed to grab the reins. The second time, I was nearly charged by water buffalo whilst trekking through a rainforest in

Malaysia. It was on my first honeymoon, and even the trip there was an adventure. We had boarded a National Express coach and headed to the Airport. Halfway into our journey, disaster struck. The windshield of the bus just exploded into millions of tiny pieces. We had been in a crash on the M25 rush hour.

I think I can smell myself, and it doesn't seem pleasant.

"Alexa set reminder 930 am. Shower."

I think I can finally sleep now. Ginger, Rex, and the gang seemed to have settled down a little, just the headache and buzzing. I must remind myself to drink the water by my bed. I ask the wife.

"Do we have any Aspirin?"

I have woken up covered in sweat from head to toe, and It's taken me about half an hour to get out of my pit.

"Head, shoulders, knees and toes, knees and toes. Head, shoulders, knees and toes, knees and toes and eyes and ears and mouth and nose. Head, shoulders, knees and toes knees and toes."

It looks okay outside, so perhaps we can fit in a trip to see the Otters. Just have to sort the rugby on later.

There is not much moving outside yet; however, the sun only just come up. I guess it's still early. A few joggers and the wrens back skirting from tree to tree, but still too fast for my camera. Ronnie and Reggie, the magpie twins, are still not about. They have been building a new nest, but they seem to have abandoned it. The squirrels are running around. It's time for a cuppa. The wife tells me I need to "de-tramp" myself today. Haircut, shave, and definitely a shower. I will have one later. I'm too tired right now. My head's buzzing.

The Void would be a good name for a superhero.

Have you ever heard the phrase?

"Call of the void"

The easiest way I can describe it is this.

"The impulse to hurl yourself into a void. Jumping off high places. To suddenly swerve your car into a lane of traffic next to you. To scream at the top of your voice on a crowded bus".

It's actually quite a common thing and has nothing to do with Mental Health, believe it or not. Every car that drives by, I think of throwing myself under. Every bridge or carpark, the feeling I wish I was up there, ready to jump into the void. I feel like that all the time. I think it's a good name.

"I am the VOID"

That can be my superhero's name. I so wish I could fly. I don't think I can, so I must remember not to test this theory. On the plus side, my NHS app tells me I don't have prostate cancer. At least, I think that's what it says. I feel a little gutted, if I'm honest. That could have been my way out. Oh well, I may have to rely on the brain tumour I have now. I must have one hiding in there somewhere.

The dog wants his belly rubbed, and social media feeds are full of St Patrick's Day celebrations and memes. The many adverts referring to things I have googled over the last few days. I swear I'm being watched and listened to. The Huusk knives look good, though. I was only saying to the wife the other day we could do with some new kitchen knives. Anyway, it's time to get up and get dressed and get out to see the Otters. I'm going to have a shave later, and a shower, so I may just as well put the clothes on that are in the corner. Another day won't hurt.

I like being out in nature, looking at the birds, the Otters, and the wildlife. I think it's really helping me. Unfortunately, the void is always with me. How deep is the water? How do you drown? Do I just jump in and start breathing, taking in water and filling my lungs?

How does it work? What would it feel like to breathe in water? How long would it take?

I'm not sure about drowning myself. Well, not unless I'm strapped to some breeze blocks. The train sounds good, or the car park the taller one. The top left flat balcony on the David Murray John Tower. I wish I could turn my brain off. It's so draining.

The wife wants to go out and have breakfast somewhere. I'm not hungry, so I will probably just have something later, a few crab sticks, maybe whilst watching the rugby. I have no idea what we can do for dinner. I can't be bothered. I don't even want to go outside, if I'm honest. I'm happy looking out the window all day. Maybe the distraction of the Otters will drown out the ringing noise, but I don't feel like getting out of bed today.

I can see his friend's face greeting us at the races. The man in the corner by the light. People hugging me and giving me money. The green and white striped waistcoat. When will it stop? I don't know how much more I can take.

My life is very black-and-white at the moment. If it says don't ride on the footpath, then you shouldn't be riding on the footpath. If the speed limit says 20, then you go 21, maybe 22 at a push, but no more. I even complained about a meal at a Harvester restaurant once when we were in Torquay. I ordered a full rack of ribs, but when it turned up, it was tiny. I called the waiter over to ask him where the rest of my food was.

"You advertised a full rack of ribs. That's a minimum of ten pieces. I've got six. It's almost 50% less than what it should be."

He told me that's what head office sends them. I even wrote an email to the head office, but I'm still waiting for a response. The story of my life was really just someone else letting me down in some way. To me, life is simple at the moment you hold doors open for a woman.

You help the old lady in the shops and say Hello, Please and Thank you. You smile and wave, just smile and wave.

My ears are ringing like mad level 8. My wife said I looked sad. The truth is it's more than that. I'm everything: sad, angry, upset, disappointed, numb, hollow, ashamed and afraid. Car Park, Train, or Window. Shall I take my pills tonight? I hope not taking them will kill me in the night. It's all making me feel suicidal. I don't want to be feeling like this. I can't put up with it anymore. It's doing my head in. I'm not a survivor. I'm barely surviving. I want to thrive, not just survive. I want to do it for my wife and for my family, for all the people helping me. I want you to do it for me!

The birds, the Otters, the fishing. This is just a moment that's going to pass, and as long as I keep heading north, I'm going to be alright no matter how many twists and turns along the way. Sometimes, it gets a little too tough. I've never hurt myself, but it's quite common for people with Mental Health problems to self-harm to cut themselves. That's not for me, thank you. I don't want to cut myself; I don't need more scars, and it is dangerous. It could kill me, and that's not the way I wish to go.

I don't self-harm, not physically anyway, although sometimes I don't bother taking my medication. Hopefully, I will get a blood clot on my brain tonight. I can't be bothered anymore. I already know my haematology doctor is going to moan at me again. They can always tell when I'm not taking my drugs. It's going to be another hospital appointment for me again soon to drain some more blood out. I know my wife's going to kill me when she reads that part, but at the start of my book, I talk about helping someone, how that person is me. I would never tell my wife I haven't been taking my pills, and I hope it kills me. That's the talk of a madman. Putting it down on paper and being totally honest with what I'm writing is how this book is going to help me. Just please, love, don't shout at me, don't moan and hate me. Don't tell me you can't do this anymore. Believe it or not, I need you right now, and I know how upsetting this is. I love you.

Hopefully, tomorrow, I will be better, and we can try again.

The good thing is I have your support

I finally managed to capture a picture of the wren flying around my garden. This was taken not long after sunrise. The wren is the most common bird in the UK and has a beautiful voice, I love nature

Chapter Ten
The High Commissioners Son

My parents moved to Egypt when I was in my twenties. It was a mad time. The number of drugs I had in my system was crazy, always trying to find a way through this battle raging on inside my head. It was great when I went to visit them both. Me and Mummy went to visit the pyramids and the museum; I love ancient Egypt. It fascinates me, and I've even got some Egyptian artifacts in my little collection.

We used to go to the country club. Dream Land was a way out in the desert. What an oasis it was, lush green grass, swimming pools, and amazing golf courses. Stunningly amazing golf courses with the lushest green grass you have ever seen right in the middle of the desert. I was playing a round of golf with my dad one day. We were only just starting out in the game; however, Dad comes to play golf here all the time. We got onto one of the holes, and he started telling me about the last time he was here. He hit an awful tee-shot. It ended up going for a swim. The caddies around erupted into laughter.

"Gamousa Gamousa."

My dad, who is a little bigger than me, shouted back.

"Oi, I know what that means."

Before making the sound of a buffalo, complete with fingers for horns. When you go to work overseas, golf is about the only thing to do, and everyone plays it.

Dad loves his golf, and so does mum. They used to be out there all the time. I really enjoyed visiting them and going out for a round. The only thing I hated about the golf courses in the middle of the desert was the bloody flies. I couldn't stand it; they covered you the minute you stood still.

I've played golf at Minahouse in front of the pyramids and may have even put a ball over the wall on the left a few times, but as we didn't hear a smash, we presumed all was good. Not that the locals would have cared much. Some of the public transport buses had wheels missing. Some of the locals would even cut their own arms and legs off in the hope that they could beg for more money out on the streets. The hope is that people feel sorrier for them than the normal beggars.

They would always go to the country club at the weekends. All coworkers for the company Dad managed. We would pile into the minibus and head off. My dad's chauffeur would always be the one driving. This one day, we all loaded the van and headed out, zooming down the motorway. Sawat slammed on the brakes quickly and pulled over onto the side of the road. It was probably equivalent to the M25 but with twice as many cars, and it didn't even matter if they were on the wrong side of the road!

Sawat disappeared for about five minutes, then came back.

"What's wrong?"

People were asking.

"Police checkpoint ahead. They have spotters looking out for people speeding. Then radio ahead saying stop white minibus full of English. Then big fine and maybe lose my job."

"So, what did you do?"

Came a response from my dad.

"Paid them to let us through."

That was simply his reply as if it were an everyday occurrence.

We drove half a mile ahead, and the road was already clear, so we could drive straight on. To the side of the pop-up checkpoints were about ten policemen, semi-automatic machine guns by their sides. Standing waving to us and nodding their heads with big smiles.

There was a garden party at the British Embassy we were invited to, so again, with Sawat at the wheel, we headed off.

As we were driving, someone shouted out

"We're going the wrong way."

Sawat was on autopilot, taking us to the Country Club.

"Embassy, Embassy, we are going to the Embassy."

Shouted my dad.

"Sorry, Sorry, No problem."

He pulled over to the side of the road and looked behind him. With a crunch of the gears and an arm over the passenger seat, it was left-hand drive. Sawat started reversing. I was sat in the back so I could see all that was going on.

"Stop, Stop for Fuck Sake. CAR CARRRRRR!"

He reversed back through the joining motorway traffic. Back over the junction he had just missed, cars were flying at us from everywhere, and I honestly thought that was it. I'm gone. Hundreds of beeping horns later and the odd screech of tyres on the tarmac. We made it back to the junction, and even today, I have no idea how we survived that. We did, however arrive at the Embassy safely, and I won five coconuts on the shy.

Mum and Dad lived in an area called Maadi. They had a lovely big house and a beautiful garden with armed sentry points on pretty much every corner. It was great because there was a McDonald's at the end of the road where I used to go grab some lunch dressed in my T-shirt and shorts. The locals all dressed in woolly hats, gloves, and puffer jackets.

I think I stared at them just as much as they were staring at me, probably thinking the same too,

"Look at that idiot, the way he is dressed in this weather."

It was their winter at the time, but I found it very pleasant.

My parents had a housemaid called Hanni. He was a great guy, totally bonkers. Hanni wanted to show me the real Cairo and how the Egyptians really lived, and I was well up for it.

We both left the house and walked up to a bus stop. I offered to treat him to a McDonalds, but he had other plans.

This noisy, knackered old thing pulled up, and we boarded. I was just glad it had all its wheels, to be honest. Everyone was staring at me. It was weird. We took a seat behind a middle-aged gentleman who nodded his head, and I spoke.

"Hello"

In Arabic. He just kept smiling at me. I could see his teeth and a huge, welcoming smile. He nods his head up and down, just smiling.

"Salaam Aleikum"

"Aleikum Salaam"

I presumed it was his little son who was sat next to him. He was a young lad with short black hair, maybe 7 or 8 years old. He is wearing a pair of shorts with no top. We spent the entire trip into the centre of the city with the little lad just staring at me with his mouth open. Never once looking away or changing his expression. I kept smiling and nodding at him, saying hello, but he didn't move.

We had a wander around for a bit through market stalls and squares with everyone staring, trying to invite you in and have a seat. We stopped at a restaurant. Well, I don't know what else to call it. It looked rougher than "Kats Café," and that's when Ozzy had it. The menu wasn't great as you didn't have a choice. He wanted to show me how the locals ate. It was a dive of a place, with lots of seating and tables.

There was a man sitting a few yards away from me, eating his food with his fingers and just staring at me. Hanni paid for my meal, and we had water to drink from a metal cup. This was his treat to me. I fancied a kebab, if I'm honest, but I couldn't believe the price, considering everyone seemed so poor. A formed metal tray was placed in front of me with what looked like different types of curries and bread. It was mainly lentils, and I loved it. Not really, but that's what I told Hanni.

He wanted to show me something special and wonderful to him, so we started to head to the Mosque of Al-Hussein.

Hanni had explained to me that when we go in, we have to be quiet and respectful. We have to hand our shoes to the man at the front desk, and being a foreigner, I would have to pay $1 to get them back.

"That's fine"

I agreed. It was such a beautiful place filled with worshippers and sounds. We walked around for about fifteen minutes, with Hanni explaining to me how people pray. I didn't take any of it in. I just kept staring at some of the people, praying they had massive scars on their foreheads.

"The ones with the blood. These are the really religious ones."

He explained. We approached the man at the front desk, so I grabbed my wallet out to pay for my shoes. I handed over $5 as that's the lowest note I had. The place erupted, and the man at the front desk started shouting at Hanni and loud at the top of his voice. Hanni was screaming back at the attendant, whose arms were flying everywhere. I just stood there thinking, what the hell is going on?

By now, there must have been about 30 people surrounding me and Hanni, all shouting, all waving their arms around like they were at a rave! Hanni tried desperately to shout the loudest. He came over to me, pushing his way through the sea of people surrounding us.

"They think you are rich because you gave them $5 and not $1. They now want more money to let you go. Don't worry. I have told them you have paid five times as much already, so you won't be paying them anymore. I have also told them they better let us go as you are the High Commissioner's Son."

I nearly fainted. I was Fucked!

"What the FUCK did you say that for?"

"It's ok we can go. Come get your shoes."

I thought I was going to be kidnapped and held to ransom. Hopefully, they would pay up, or my head would be cut off. I decided it would be a good idea to go home now. Hanni wanted to stay out, but I've had enough excitement for one night.

I have been back to Egypt several times and loved it. I've picked up a few phrases and words, and it's still funny when I talk Arabic in the hotels. The locals can't believe it either. They are amazed by it.

"Hello, how are you today? Can I have two drinks of vodka and coke with no ice, please? Thank you very much. I hope you have a good evening."

I did get warned by a lifeguard once, though. I was talking away around the pool to some sales rep, trying to get me to go scuba diving or something. The lifeguard said to me.

"I see you speak Arabic. Why is this?"

"I think it's important that when I come to your country. I learned some of your language. Just a little, just enough to say Please and Thank you. To me, it's a sign of respect."

"My friend, you must not do this if a white man is speaking Arabic. This means he is rich and lives in a big house in Cairo. Many people will not like this. So, you must stop. I beg you, it is for your own safety."

This guy had a huge scar on his face, running from top to bottom. My wife banned me from talking in Arabic for the rest of the holiday. Although I did slip in a few words every now and then, just the odd,

"Hello" and "Thank you, I hope you have a good evening".

Most people don't like places like Egypt. I love it. The people are mainly very, very friendly. Ok, you might get eaten by a shark, but have you checked out some of the monsters in the UK waters?

A tenner at the start of your holiday to the barman at your favourite bar goes a long way, trust me. We found a lovely beach bar in our hotel complex. We would spend the evenings just watching the stars, and not once did we go to the bar to order any drinks. At the start of this trip, I spoke with the barman.

"As-salami Alaykum"

The way I pronounce it is *salam, al e kum*

The reply I got with a huge smile across this young man's face.

"As-salami alaykum, you speak Arabic!"

Again, the reverse is Al e kum, salam

So basically, I just said hello, and he replied with hello back. That's the simple version, anyway. It means peace be upon you, and the reply is always peace be on you, too. To be honest, if we all had that kind of mantra, I think the world could be a better place.

I'm not into religion, but that doesn't mean you can't be. Yes, there are crazy parts in all religions, no matter what God or thing you believe in. That's your belief, and you are entitled to it. My beliefs are so wacky, but yet, at the moment, that's truly what my head believes. My belief system at the moment thinks someone's going to attack and try to kill me; I don't know who you are or where you are, but you're hiding somewhere, and I think it's close. That's the hypervirulence coming out again. It's always there day in and day out. I can stand at my window for hours just looking, staring at everything that moves. On high alert Defcon One. Every sound is a potential threat that needs scrutinising. How I'm going to escape and defend myself against one of the Gargoyles that could attack at any second. I'm the same when I'm out. Everywhere I go requires a thorough risk assessment. Everywhere I go, scanning for dangers, and I constantly wish I had ED-209 by my side.

I'm in the supermarket. It's not that busy, so this could work in my favour. I can see several exits, so no matter which way I run, I can escape. Ideally, it's the entrance I came in. It leads to the car park where I'm parked, pretty much the same spot every time. It's not the best escape route as the security station is there. It's minded today by a massive dude with a shaved head. He looks like he was in the SAS for years. He would be my last major line of defence. I'm not too worried about him, though. I can take care of myself. I'm six foot one and built like a brick shit house. I've taken care of him many times in my head. I know how to defeat him, if needed, of course.

I have this thing called disassociation, so my field of vision is gone. All I can see is my small view of the world. It's like you're looking through a fish-eye lens. You're focusing on a small spot in the middle, maybe 10 meters ahead at all times.

The old lady won't be a problem; one kick and she would go down. The lady with the pushchair's not going to do anything but run If I need to charge her. I'm getting close to the end of the aisle now, and I need to go right. I've already mapped the store out on previous visits, so I know where everything is, what shelf it's on, left or right, top and bottom. I just hope no one stands in my way. If they do, I can go through the staff door, which leads to the warehouse.

Having never made it this far, I'm not sure what I'm going to find, but it's going to have a loading dock somewhere. Let's hope it's open. The good news is there will have to be emergency exits everywhere. If I can keep running, I will escape at some point.

"Hello"

I'm not sure how old she was, maybe in her late seventies. She had a nice smile, and I have a lot of time for old people.

"Hello, how are you today?"

Softly spoken with a nice greeting smile on my beaming face.

"Oh, lovely weather we are having."

"Yes, it is lovely outside today. I think it's going to rain later this week, but it's good for the garden, and my roses could do with it."

She seemed so pleased with my answer about my roses that we ended up having a five-minute conversation about roses and flowers we had in our gardens. It really was a pleasure meeting you that day. If only you knew.

"If you take one more step towards me or charge at me in any way, I'm going to smash you over the head with this 500-gram glass bottle of Asda's Light Mayonnaise".

My escape plan, if she charges me or makes one attempt, is first blood. I'm reaching down to grab the large jar of mayonnaise that's on the shelf to my left. I've rehearsed the moves already. She's going to get a good Whack around the head with it, then I can run.

I desperately wish I had them blood-soaked bandages back. Covering the wounds that you can't see. The pain that's going through my body right now is so evident, the wires and the tubes sticking out of me, blood gushing from the hole in my neck, spraying your trolley, covering you in my bright red sticky blood. I never would hurt you.

That's the strange thing: I'm not about going around beating up old ladies or anyone else. I'm just scared, so very scared of everyone, even if it doesn't look like it.

One of the hardest things about having a Mental Health condition is the fake smile. I love talking to people. It feels great talking about anything. Roses in my garden to what species of fish are in my local lake. What birds have I seen over the last few days, and where to spot them. The beaming smile on my face as we chatted away. People do not know the real me hiding inside. Just look at Robin Williams! Have you ever met such a happier person in your life, even if I didn't like Mork & Mindy! Unfortunately, no matter how many times you rub Aladdin's lamp and no matter how many wishes you get, you can never bring anyone back from the dead.

At this moment in my life, I'm trying to be the best possible human being I can be. I don't always get it right, but I have to understand that's how my brain is protecting me. It does what it does because it has to survive. The old saying.

"Your head is like a filling cabinet. Your files are all messed up at the moment. They just need a little help and time to get them back in order. But they will".

When people say to me how are you feeling, my general reply is.

"My heads fucked!"

I'm so sorry for overthinking like crazy again. I'm sure I was talking about religion. I don't believe in God, and I'll explain why. God has never, in my opinion, been there for me. Every time I've asked him for help or to show me a sign, it never comes. All that's happened in my life is he, or she has tried to kill me over and over and over again. The number of times I've looked up at the heavens and said in my head.

"Please, God, help me. My head's fucked right now, and I could do with some help. Please show me a sign, anything. Just to show me you're up there listening. Thank you. Oh, and can you let me win the lottery at the weekend. Thank you again. And if I win, I will give some to charity and really help people. Thank you, God."

I don't believe in God because the sciences tell me not to, and I believe in the science. I believe in the facts, the proven facts. Total black-and-white thinking.

If I could write a manual on how to deal with Mental Health, then the secret to this silent illness would be unveiled.

Sadly, Mental Health is not like this. We are all different and unique in our own ways. What I might be going through might be totally different to you. Just because I have a plague of locusts living between my ears doesn't mean you will. You might have a bumble bee nest deep inside that crazy head of you. It might last a week; it may last a month or two, maybe even six. Maybe years.

I get very tired to the point of physical exhaustion, not because I have gone on a ten-mile run. My brain just does not stop, and it's draining absolutely fucking draining, sorry for my language. Find something you like to do, like I've said for me, that's fishing and birdwatching. For you, it could be the same, maybe reconnect with things you did as a kid. I love my collection of toys, the ones that I played with as a child. Honestly, I beg you to try it. Sit on the floor as you did as a child.

I was playing the other day, lying on the rug in my living room. The General Lee was skidding around, jumping over a broken bridge, spinning and twisting in the air. It was trying to get away from the marauding gang of plastic dinosaurs that were all converging on its location. With a quick step on the gas, a billowing cloud of dust and burning rubber rises up. Bo and Luke smile and laugh at each other as they escape, but little do they know the Stay-Puff Marsh Mellow Man was about to pounce.

My wife came in whilst I was playing, and she could see how much fun I was having. She even wanted to join in.

Try it, go on. It's fun. If you can afford to, then go buy a toy that means something to you. Hold it in your hands. How does it feel? What it's made of?

Make one of them parachute men. We all have a drawer full of them bags for life. This will make the canopy of the parachute, cut a large circle on one of the sides. Tie four pieces of string or cotton equally around it, all leading down to a weight of some sort. A piece of stick, maybe, tie that on. Now, gently roll it all up and go outside. Give it a good chuck as high in the air as you can.

It might take a little practice, but you will get the hang of it. I can't remember if you need to cut a small hole in the top of the bag, so if it doesn't fall like a parachute, try that.

Connect with that inner child of yours. It can be a very fun and relaxing place to be. My sister tells me I shouldn't waste my money on toys and crap. Little does she know the true joy they bring me. These toys are helping me right now, and I love them. They have become a solid foundation for me to build on. They keep me anchored into the ground.

Like I was saying, I'm a man of science, and that's why I don't believe in God. Think about it: God created the world around 4500 BC. But the world has been around for billions of years, science proven!

How can you create a world if that world already exists?

That's like me saying I've just created a new chocolate bar, and it's called Mars! Evolution is a proven thing. I'm sure you don't want me to ramble on, as this book is probably more boring than I think. Just to say, though, I have figured out not only the world but the entire universe and how the place we call Space happened. The Big Bang, why it happened, everything I have documented. Come on, Professor Brian Cox, reply to that email I sent you.

I may be crazy, but it's something you need to listen to. Right, rant over back to the book again!

I have to admit I haven't read the Bible. I might do it one day just out of interest, but I can't help but think about how it is written. To me, it should be more like a diary.

Saturday 15th February 1250

"Just popped down to the beach earlier. Met up with this dude called Moses. I kid you not, he waved his hands, and the sea just parted. It happened right in front of my eyes. Anyway, we are going to meet up again later. He's doing some gardening and wants a hand cleaning some scrubland and moving some bushes around.

Pete caught a beautiful fish earlier, so we are going to have a BBQ with some foraged leaves and a tangy mushroom sauce."

My wife was worried about going to Egypt. She thought she would get the runs, but my top tip is this. Avoid the local water, which also has to include the fruit and veg its mainly water, fruits and vegetables are made up mainly entirely of water. Yeah, the hotels might wash them before cooking or serving, but it's still made of water. It's a poor country. Farmers aren't going to use bottled mineral water on their crops in a desert. The locals would have built up an immune system to it all. Not us Westerners, so stick to the meat.

Having said all that, my wife does owe 50 Euros even though not all of it's on the floor, and I'm not the High Commissioner's son!

Minahouse Golf Course right in the Centre of Cairo City.

First tee was always a challenge. A massive wall on the left, all out of bounds. The other side of the wall was the main road with hundreds of cars and three wheeled buses!

"Salam Alaikum"

I love visiting Egypt the people are so friendly, mostly!

**Chapter Eleven
Overthinking**

Overthinking is shit; I hate it. You literally can't switch your brain off. It's constantly going. It doesn't matter what you're doing, where you are, or who you are with. It just keeps going like that bloody bunny. I can't remember a time that I didn't overthink things. I try thinking about it sometimes, but it's a question I simply can't answer. Just by logic, thinking about thinking is just thinking about thinking things or just simply overthinking things. If I overthink things, then how do I know if I'm just thinking or overthinking things? Am I right to think about overthinking? Should I try not to think about overthinking, or will that trigger me into more overthinking? I need to think of something to stop my overthinking about overthinking thinking conversation. I may start to overthink. Am I doing it now? I don't think I am. No, I must be, and believe me, some of the things I think about are weird.

The other days, I was a time traveller living hundreds of years in the past. I was thinking of how my ancient Egyptian Signet Ring and Armlets were worn and by whom.

Were you wearing them whilst building the pyramids? Probably with a little help from them above. I've always wondered about the speed of light and the connection to the pyramids!

Someday, I go way into the future, a time when little remains of the Earth, and we've ended up killing ourselves. The Nuclear Apocalypse 2273. The population of the planet has exploded exponentially, unemployment is rife, and poverty is everywhere to be seen. People are fighting over what little food there is left. Race wars will start out religious wars. Whole countries are persecuted and destroyed just for believing in a different god. A god that most people will probably be needing in these harsh Mad Max times. Countries and continents will fight for what little resources are left till, eventually, resulting in the ultimate price, the destruction of our planet. I know you think I am a complete idiot, but seriously, what does it look like in your head? What's your picture of the end of the world?

And if I'm totally honest with you, I wish it would happen today!

Do you even bother thinking about it? It's not like we are going to be around to care. It's going to be in millions of years anyway. The truth is if we carry on the way we are, it won't be that long at all. I'm not an eco-warrior, and I don't go around annoying half the general population by wearing an orange vest. I don't know the date it's going to happen, and chances are I'm not a real-time traveller, but we will all be in a Mad Max society one day, and it's not science fiction. It's a science fact. Life will continue. Those little cockroaches I played with as a kid will multiply, safely living out the nuclear winters. With the acid rains billions of years from now, the world will be a different place. Evolution is doing what it does best: creating a new species. Technically, humans like us. I don't know if they will look like little grey men or like one of them bugs from Starship Troopers, but you have to remember it's happened before. If that rock hadn't of hit the planet all them billions of years ago, then the dinosaurs would still be walking the Earth today, and you wouldn't be wondering why the hell you bought this book!

I like nature; nature's good. The birds singing, the butterflies and bees buzzing around. The fish swimming in the flow of the pond, the sound of the waterfalls. I'm a massive advocate for getting outside as much as you can. I try to get out when I can, although some days are easier than others, so just listen to what your body needs and what it is telling you. It's a pretty smart device. It got you this far in life. Just trust it. It's trying to protect you. Some days, I spend all day in bed just staring out the window. Just sat watching the flies buzzing around the pane of glass in front of me. Just staring at them, thinking to myself, why don't you just fly out, you stupid things? The window is open. Just go, God, they are so dumb!

I'm watching these flies buzzing around like crazy. The noise inside their heads must be deafening, but one I can relate to.

"BUZZZZZZZZZZZZZZZZZZZZZZZZZZZZZZZZZZZZZZZZZ ZZZZZZZZZZZZZZZZZZZZZZZZZZZZZZZZZZZZZZZZZZZZZ ZZZZZZZZZZZZZZZZZZZZZZZZZZZZZZZZZZZZZZZZZZZZZ"

"Look, that's where you need to go. The window is open. Just fly through it. It's easy!"

I suddenly twig that with all that buzzing noise going on and rattling their brains around, they simply don't know which way is up or down, left or right. They can clearly see what's in front of them.

"The sky is right there in front of you, the outside world where you can be free."

But that invisible force field keeps holding you back, stopping you from reaching the other side. That invisible clear pane of glass that lets you see the world, it's like you are almost a part of it in some way, but it feels distant, so very distant and far away. That little part of the world you are trapped in is holding you back in some way. Everything and everyone else in the World is just passing you by, not even looking. If only they knew you needed a helping hand. But it's not easy when the buzzing keeps going off. I'm not sure if flies are social animals or how they communicate with each other if at all they do. I wonder if they had someone else they could talk to and ask for help. A friend, a teacher, anyone. I'm sure if they asked their friends for help, they would figure it out and find a way. At the moment, that pane of glass is stopping you from getting to freedom even though the windows open.

If only I could figure out what way is Up and what way is Down, what was is Left and which was is Right. Only then will I be able to break through and be free once again?

I might only manage a few words today, but that's good enough for me. Tomorrow, I can get out, maybe a little walk around the lake, maybe see if I can't get a rod in the water. I could get there early, at sunrise, and stay till sunset and hunt down a 20lb plus carp. Let's see what happens. I do have to get up at some point, though, as I haven't had a shower in a week.

"And you can get your arse in the shower today. What's it been a week. And don't think that thing's coming near me till you do."

I love my wife, and believe it or not, that's the encouragement I need right now. Our sex life has gone downhill a bit, if I'm honest. We started our relationship like rabbits, and that's carried on for years. Nowadays, it might be every other week. I do wake up with a horn on some mornings, but sometimes, it doesn't feel like the right moment. It's also the Erectile Dysfunction that does it for me. Another problem that can arise, or not in my case, because of my Mental Health issues. Guess I'm not going to win any awards this time. I've got from a solid 9 inches to a floppy seven!

There's a blackbird that's just flown into the garden. It's black in colour, so it's a male. He's just got onto one of the waterfalls and is having a bath. He visits every day; he comes and eats his breakfast, his lunch, and his dinner here. I really should take a leaf out of nature's book. I'm sitting in the garden right now writing my book, but I've needed to take about four months off as it just hasn't felt right, and my head's all over the place. I'm sitting in my garden. It's another of my happy places, I wish you could see it. I love it so much. It is a place where I can come and relax when needed.

We don't argue often, but I had a row with the wife the other day, and that wasn't nice. I also need to order a new remote control for the TV, this one won't work anymore. I guess it didn't appreciate being thrown against the wall.

I needed to get out of the house just to get away and clear my head.

"If you leave, then that's it. We are over!"

I shut the door and walked off, heading to the lake, my safe Ish spot. A very lonely walk that's surrounded by darkness and ringing everywhere. The tunnel vision and the kaleidoscope effect are going on in my head. Every step is hard to take, and every breath is difficult to control. It's a really dark night, and the stars are out. There is a blind bend in the road with very few street lights around; it's a very gloomy night.

"Lie down in the middle of the road. You're dressed in black. The cars won't see you, not until it's too late."

"But I will hear them coming."

"Not all cars make a noise, you know, go on, lie down. You can do it. Lie down for me. Trust me, take my hand."

I walked on and took a seat on the bench, looking at the water over my lake, watching the reflections of the trees and the moon on its mill pond surface.

"Wade in. Go and lie down in the middle of the lake. Start breathing under the water. You can do it, I know you can do it, it's easy, just start breathing, join me."

"But it's too shallow. I can stand up?"

"Just try it. Trust me."

I took out my phone and removed a credit card-sized piece of plastic from the case. I sat there crying for ten minutes, thinking about what messages I wanted to leave my family.

I couldn't do it. The pictures of my wife and my children, the last words I wanted to tell them.

My wife was not happy when I got home, but we talked and talked for hours. I opened up more, and it felt good to have her there by my side. So many tears that night, lots of tears.

God, my life is a nightmare right now. I so want to get better for my family and my children. It's just a little difficult right now. I live my life and view it standing about 4 inches behind myself. Stick a toilet plunger to your head and walk around the house. Keep staring at the end of the plunger whilst walking. It's not that easy, is it? That's how I would describe it. It feels weird. I'm not worried about it too much. Don't get me wrong, sometimes it really pisses me off, but you get used to it, kind of. Meditation helps Binomial Music and some reverse breathing. Why don't you give that a go?

My wife has just come and joined me in the garden. She works from home, up in her office. It's great for me as I spend most of my days hiding in the bedroom. The office isn't far away, so I can hear her and see her most of the time. It's comforting knowing she is close, and she doesn't like leaving me on my own, just in case.

We are sitting in the garden, relaxing and talking.

"He must have been crapping himself after I got away.

Was I going to say anything?

Was I going to hide his secrets?

What he and his friends have done to me."

He is in my head all the time. I just want you out somehow. Someway, just go, please.

People have hurt me all my life. That's how I feel; that's my belief, and that's why I'm too scared to go out of my house. I try to get out, but it's hard, especially when it's somewhere new. It's too much for me.

He is with me sometimes; I might be in the bedroom listening to relaxing music, trying to chill out and relax. I have to get under the covers and close the windows as he stands by the side of my bed, watching me, always wearing the same uniform he wore at the nursing home. He watches over me, smiling. I can feel him touching me, placing his hands on my waist. I can hear him talking to me. We don't have conversations, he just says.

"Hello"

With a huge smile across his face. Close the windows and pull the sheets over your head. He might get in. Anyone might get in.

"Where are they?"

"Who are they?"

Is it him, was he one of them, is he going to hurt me?

If he tries, what can I do about it? How can I defend myself?

Don't get me wrong, I haven't always been a saint in my life. I've been a proper twat with some of the things I've done. I'm sure we all have, but I didn't deserve this. I was a young, naive boy, not very street-wise and very, very immature. You played on that; you made me your friend. I loved playing games with you. I loved spending time on the computer playing all those new games. That jet fighter joy sticks with a million buttons. Working together at the nursing home, the Polo Club and Cheltenham Races was the best time of my life. Just me and my only true friend. I'm thinking about this really hard at the moment. Should I forgive you for the abuse I suffered at your hands and the hands of all your friends?

How can I forgive you for what you have done to me? You set out on your mission to make me your plaything. You knew what you wanted from the start. It wouldn't surprise me if you have honed your skills over a long period of time. I know there are more friends of yours. You told me!

How many people are hiding behind this man's name?

People say you need to be able to forgive what happened in some way, to move on from all of this, but I can't at the moment. It's not because I don't want to. It's because it's in my head. As yet, I haven't had the correct chance to process it all. To figure out what file goes where. Where does paragraph 2, page 62 need to go?

This book is helping me put everything back in order, and I'm sure that by reading it, you can see I have a little way to go!

That's why things in this book probably do not make a lot of sense. If someone can come along and explain to me the step-by-step process that I need to take in order to get through this in a logical, scientific manner, then I think there may be hope for me.

Many people who have gone through trauma often think about writing a story or have indeed done that. Some will keep their stories on the bedside table. Some will burn them after it's completed or even partway through. For me, it's helped to get pen to paper or fingers on keyboard.

I have got a little better at typing and can use about 4 fingers at wonce now. However, I'm still totally rubbish at spelling. You should see all the red and blue squiggly lines running down the page. Got to love a bit of spell check.

Listen, at the end of the day, it doesn't matter how well we can read and right. It doesn't matter if the spelling and punctuation are. not there., The first draft of my book was pretty much one long sentence. If it helps you, then why not give it a go? It's not easy to write your story. So many triggers and so many thoughts go through your head. I've had to take months off; it can become too much, so keep an eye on your window of tolerance.

Make sure you do enough so you feel you have achieved something today, even if that's just reading a few lines back or adding a chapter or two. Leaving it on the hard drive for a day, a week, or a month. Whatever you need, just take it at a pace you can cope with.

I have had a few people look over my book. So they can give me their opinion on whether they think it might help others. The main feedback I get is about how honest I have been. This is my story, and I have to write it how I see it. Write your story how you see it; be honest in it, though.

My story had been hidden for decades. It fucked me up big time. Forgiveness: I can't forgive you at the moment. How can I forgive you for betraying me? I thought we were best friends. Friends don't lie! It's taken thirty-odd years to say that. I'm glad I did. Hiding this away for so long it has really affected me now. The trauma builds up for all those years. I always knew it wasn't right what he was doing to me. I just wanted a friend. When I did finally get out and for the next thirty years, I have thought about it. Overthought it so many times. Talking away in my head.

"Was he my friend?"

"Did you care about me?"

When I found myself working in the area, I would drive down the road and park outside his house, wondering if he was still there. What he would be doing and how he might look. I have no idea why I did it. I was hoping he was dead.

Counselling helps, and talking has helped me tremendously. But it can sometimes be frustrating; you sit there talking about your feelings. I love that part, and I'm more than happy to talk now. They tell you to be honest. One of my counsellors asked me.

"What would you do if he was in the room with you right now?"

"Fucking kill him. Skin the Cunt alive!"

"That's not what I really want to hear!"

Sorry, but you asked for the truth. If you don't want to hear it, then don't ask the question.

I bumped into him once. It was at the local corner shop. The place I used to get the games from as a kid. I was walking from my van, mainly reminiscing about the place and how it looked after all these years when he walked out and up the steps; I knew it was him instantly. Coming out of the little corner shop where he bought all those games many years ago. With a plastic bag and a bottle of sherry.

"Hello, Robbie"

With a huge smile on his face.

I just walked past, head down, saying to myself.

"He's not been caught yet. What do I do. What will I do if he is still outside waiting for me?"

I spent ages walking around that tiny little shop, just reminiscing. When I googled his name, the realisation of what he did, hit me like a freight train. I knew what it was, but he told me no one would ever believe me. I trusted him, so I had no reason to disbelieve this.

I told you overthinking was shit. I've overthought this entire chapter.

I'm glad I did.

A garden visitor today, a friendly Blackbird.

He comes most days for breakfast, lunch and dinner. He loves to stand on the edge of the waterfall and have a bath.

GLOUCESTERSHIRE COUNTY COUNCIL

ANNUAL REPORT

NAME:- ▓▓▓▓▓▓▓▓▓▓ YEAR: 3.
DATE:- June 1986 TEACHER:- ▓▓▓▓▓▓▓▓

GRADING SCALE

N.F.E.R. TESTS AND YEAR'S ACHIEVEMENT

The normal spread of ability within an age group should be:-
- A = 2%
- B = 14%
- C+,C, & C- = 68%
- D = 14%
- E = 2%

- A = Very Good
- B = Good
- C+,C, & C- = Average
- D = Below Average
- E = Very Weak

EFFORT
1. Always does his/her best.
2. Varies
3. Rarely does his/her best.

The letter assessment has been given to indicate the child's performance in the National Foundation for Educational Research Tests in English, Mathematics and Reading which are completed at the end of each Junior year. It is also used to give an assessment for achievement for the year's work in the subject. An assessment is also given for effort.

SUBJECT	N.F.E.R. Assessment	Assessment of year's work	
		Achievement	Effort
MATHS	96c	C-	2
ENGLISH	96c	C-	2
READING	106c+	C+	2

GENERAL COMMENT: ▓▓▓ seemed to settle quickly but he does find it difficult to concentrate for any length of time. He seems to be interested, participating well orally but he finds recording on paper, in writing, difficult. His spelling is weak as is his sentence construction. He is able to record well pictorially however and enjoys drawing. On an individual basis he is polite and pleasant but he can be disruptive and argumentative among his classmates. A keen sportsman but intolerant of other children's efforts. Work is neat but difficult to read because it is so small. Mechanical maths reasonable, but finds problem solving difficult. He also finds it difficult to set out his maths clearly. More effort and self-discipline needed next year.

Signed: ▓▓▓▓▓ Class Teacher

I am pleased ▓▓▓ has settled in well at the school. He does, however, have a number of problems he must try to come to terms with.

Signed: ▓▓▓▓▓ Headmaster.

Your child's teacher for next term will be: ▓▓▓▓▓

One of my very old school reports, I'm aged 10.

It's a little hard to read, so have a look on the next page.

Teacher Comments

Robbie seemed to settle quickly, but he does find it difficult to concentrate for any length of time. He seems to be interested participating well orally, but he finds recording on paper difficult in writing. His spelling is weak, as is his sentence construction. He is able to record well pictorially, however, and enjoys drawing. On an individual basis, he is polite and pleasant, but he can be disruptive and argumentative among his classmates. A keen sportsman but intolerant of other's childish efforts. Work is neat but difficult to read because it is so small. Mechanical maths is reasonable, but finds problem-solving difficult. He also finds it difficult to set out his maths clearly. More effort and self-discipline needed next year.

Head Teacher Notes

I am pleased Robbie has settled in well at school. He does, however, have a number of problems he must try to come to terms with

Chapter Twelve
The Otters

I've always loved otters; they are such lovely animals. Most fishermen hate them as they do eat fish; however, we have to remember it's their home and not ours, and they have more right to be there than you.

It's not a secret my Mental Health hasn't been great lately, and I'm trying to do anything and everything to get it back on track. Rejoining the fishing lake that I live near, I used to fish there over 30 years ago as a junior. It's such a lovely place to walk around. Get out in the open and see the wildlife. I can spend hours just sitting down by the lake, fishing away, watching and seeing what's happening. Listening to the birds singing away and chatting to each other. We also get Otters on the lake from time to time, but this is very rare. I need to see the Otters, though.

Luckily, a few miles down the road, I know of a lake where they live. Off we shoot to Go Outdoors to stock up on new walking boots and all-weather jackets. The plan is to stop making excuses and get out more, no matter what the weather. So here we are, sitting on the decking area next to the café, drinking hot chocolate, sprinkling marshmallows, and lashings of wiped cream.

My wife loves watching the kingfishers flying around the millions of dragonflies, all wanting to say hello. It is a lovely day, a little overcast but quite warm; even the Otters are swimming around. It looks like mum is teaching the kids how to catch fish. It looks like they are getting the hang of it, though. They would dive down, and the surface of the lake would erupt with bubbles, heading off in a line down the lake. Then, up, they would pop, roll over, and lie on their backs. Grasping a little roach between its paws. Before ripping its head off, repeating the process over and over again.

It's so magical watching these wild animals going about their daily routine just yards from the viewing platform. I've managed to get some great videos of them diving and swimming around.

I love anything nature now. It helps me so much with everything. Don't get me wrong, some days I still can't get out of bed, but you learn to take the rough with the smooth.

I can have good days where I'm able to go out for breakfast with the wife. Maybe a walk around town or go out for an evening meal. Today, she wants to go out and do something "NORMAL!". Get the bus into town and have a few drinks and a meal. Who doesn't like a good Ruby?

I'm running the question through my head. So, I ask my wife.

"Do you think I need to wear a nappy tonight? We are going out for a curry, remember? I've already taken some Imodium, but I'm not sure. What do you think?"

Some days, I can't get out of bed. I just sit there in silence, staring into space, thinking about everything but resolving absolutely diddly squats. Just staring at the flies!

It's really not good to lie in bed all day, every day, and you really have to force yourself out of your pit. Some days, I want it all to end, but the reality is I don't know when this will end. I'm sick of it all and don't want to play anymore. I would be quite happy for the world to end tomorrow. Blown up, disappear, whatever, just so long as it all stops.

I don't want to kill myself, but I don't want to live at the moment, either. I'm stuck in a never-ending cycle of mess inside my head. Will it stop, or won't it?

Let's get through today and see what tomorrow brings. So long as the sun keeps coming up every morning, then I have a chance. When tomorrow comes, let's see what happens. The day after that, then the day after that. Surely, somewhere along the way, things will start to get easier. Maybe just starts to get a little easier, a little better.

I hope to have a day where I don't think about the abuse and how I'm feeling. That all seems a long way off just yet, though. I'm trying. I really am trying. It's just very hard to live with.

I need to relax. I need to find a way to unwind and to distract myself from the pain that rages inside my head, day in, day out, morning till night. Hoping the nightmares don't begin again. The times you wake in the middle of the night, the sheets soaked in sweat. Your whole body covered in sweat.

Get up and go to the loo, returning and feeling how wet the sheets really are. Before lying back down and becoming chilly from the moisture. Wrapping yourself up in the duvet, hoping the Bogey Man doesn't come and grab that little toe sticking out from the bottom of the sheets.

I kick out sometimes and punch as well. I have even caught my wife once with a kick. It gave her a nasty bruise. In my head, I'm in a fight.

I'm in a basement with skinny metal shelves running along the walls. The walls are covered in deadly exotic animals, venomous spiders, and wasps, all manner of crawling inserts. The walls look as if they are moving, alive.

I'm waist-high in water; the whole basement is flooded.

It's very dim in here, and the only light source is coming from the stairwell in front of me, 7, maybe 8 yards away. It's my only escape. A Gargoyle suddenly appears out of a cloud of mist and smoke. He flies towards me, gaining speed along the way, smiling and laughing at me.

"Ha Ha Ha Ha"

In a creepy voice, echoes bouncing off the walls over and over, fading into the background. Then, just like that, he is gone. Vanished into thin air, right in front of my face, millimetre away. Like it has been sucked into my skull through some sort of third eye, I start to run, but I'm being held back somehow. The water has turned thick, like a treacle. I try wading as fast as I can, urging myself to make it up the stairs towards the dim light and safety.

I take a short rest at the end of the shelves and try to compose myself, urging myself on, trying to get them last few yards done. I place my left hand on the racking, then suddenly hear a noise. I look round to see where it is coming from. My head turned, and my eyes locked onto the shelf next to me. A Gigantic Crocodile suddenly Explodes out. Then takes my neck in his jaws, blood gushing and spurting from my open wounds, dragging me down into the thick, watery darkness and spinning over and over again.

That's where I punch out. I'm trying to beat it away, trying to get it off of me. I've only even beaten the Crocodile once. That's when the Shark comes. That's when I'm kicking out in my sleep, desperately kicking. Desperately hoping to kick it in the nose before it devours me, ripping me apart limb by limb.

Otters, wildlife, the outside nature can be my cure, the bird watching the fishing, the relaxation it offers me.

Even this can be a struggle, though. I went fishing the other day. I knew I was pushing my luck, if I'm honest, as I had a counselling session Monday, and they can be quite tough, so expect to have a counselling hangover for a few days after.

It's Wednesday, so I think I'm going to be okay with going fishing. I need to get out of the house and relax. I still feel tense and anxious about it, but I need to find a way to push through. Rexy and the gang can come if they need to.

I've just done something really stupid. I just uploaded a picture to the Facebook site of the fishing club. I'm worried I have given away my location and people will be able to find me now. I'm scared they are coming for me, to hurt me to kill me. The wife is coming to pick me up soon. I've made an excuse, to get her out the house. In reality I need her here now to take me home. There is someone in the bushes watching me, I don't know who they are but they are definitely watching me. I have taken a picture to show my wife, for proof. He has been there for about 10 minutes. I need to reposition my chair so I can see what's approaching.

"What if they come through the water and climb up the bank?"

Millions of things are rifling through your mind. When will my wife get here to look after me? That's what it's like. I get so paranoid. My problem is I don't know how many times I have been abused or by whom. You could be anywhere.

Do you have black hair or grey? Are you tall or short? Are you black? Are you white? How old will you be?

It feels like a sadistic game of Guess fucking Who!

But yet you are there, hiding and waiting for your moment to strike.

We have a row of mature trees behind our house. A strip of about seven meters or so. It's beautiful in the summer, you can't see another house. I'm staring out the window my heads going up and down scanning like robocop. I can hear people moving along the path past the trees. Someone is walking into the trees an old guy maybe mid-sixties with a full head of grey hair but thinning in the middle. He is wearing a blue top with long sleeves.

He's clambering over the floor that's covered in saplings and fallen branches coming towards my fence, towards my house.

"Oi what you doing?"

He climbed his way out soon after I shouted. What were you trying to do?

"Have you found me? Are you here to kill me?"

"Do you just have a weak bladder old man?"

Questions all the time, always questions. The fish will have to wait for another day.

Even now, I get scared, and it's almost a year down the line since breaking my silence. They say time is a healer, but first, I need to come to terms with what happened all them years ago. I have to understand it wasn't my fault. I have to realise I was groomed, and I didn't have any control over it. I have to learn to live with this but not let it define who I am as a person. I need to be normal, but I can't right now. I'm still too scared. My sister tells me I need to get out of victim mode. To be honest, she is probably right. But she is too close, too close to home. She has her own survivor story to tell, like most of the Grandkids. I'm stuck in abuse mode right now, so I don't want to listen. I just want this to stop and go away. Some days, I regret saying anything and wish I was still hiding it away. But the reality is I'm so glad I did shout. Even if it was 30 years too late, don't hide it. Let it go. Shout it from the rooftops if you have to.

People who have heard my story tell me It wasn't my fault what happened, I was too young to immature to know what was happening. My brain was still developing. But surely it must have been my fault because I let it happen, for so many years. Didn't I? I knew what he was doing was wrong. But it felt good to have a friend at last, A real friend. A friend to smoke with enjoy a drink with. A friend to play games with, I loved playing Dungeons and Dragons, for hours and hours, we would play Dungeons and Dragons, I loved watching the cartoon series of that as a kid.

"He was my friend. My one and only friend."

I felt special, very special. Nothing like one of them Special Needs kids at school that I used to be. I was earning lots of money and getting into fishing. I even had one of the first proper mobile phones, a Nokia 1011. What a waste of money that was. I didn't know anyone else who owned one at the time!

I was enjoying the company of the rich and the famous, the royals just strolling round. Happy times watching Harry and William playing with each other and their dad. Then the stress, how do I stop this? How do I get out?

But you keep going. It's a hold, it's a strange feeling, so hard to describe.

I was a child, The Gargoyle, my friend my one and only true friend, I feared him but I didn't want to lose him either. That's how it feels to go back, when you know you're being abused. Because you're too scared not to, you want to be somewhere else but you can't. It's not that easy to get out, the outside world doesn't seem much safer.

What would happen when people find out? How would your parents react? You would have to leave, kill yourself. No one would believe you! They would just think, you were this little gay kid. It wasn't like that; he was my friend.

Was it my fault? I let it happen, didn't I?

I've met other survivors; I just wish I was one too.

I'm ashamed to admit it, but I have so much resentment towards my sister. She was able to tell her story and I had to hide mine. Growing up I could never tell my story; I knew how much heartbreak it would bring on the family. The first time my sister took an overdose, as far as I can recall she was about 14, I'm not quite sure. I knew, with this on top of all the stress and worry for my sister, it would have killed one my parents. The abuse, them thinking they were not there for me, there for both of us, how did they not know. What kind of parents must we be. I couldn't put them through that. I guess it's entirely normal to blame ourselves.

We blame ourselves for everything we do, I knew they would blame themselves, but they have nothing to be blameful for. I had a great childhood I loved it.

As it happens waiting over 30 years didn't help either. Soon after I broke my silence my dad ended up in hospital with a dodgy heart, he's ok now though.

The guilt's the horrible part. This man went on to abuse more people and if I would have said something back then it would have stopped, He would be in prison. He would not have been able to continue his ways. I'm so sorry to the people that came after me. That they had to go through it too. I don't know how I can forgive myself for that not ever. Would I look at the person before me and think "I HATE HIM" for not speaking out, or would I feel pity on him for going through what I did at the hands of this man?

I need to remember that one of you out there, the person who told their story and broke their silence, you gave me the courage and the strength to stand up. To be heard to finally start to find a way out of this mess. I'm typing this and shouting the words in my head this very second. Shouting louder and louder like I'm Martin Luther King shouting to a crowd, I have a dream. It's a dream to be happy to let go.

I'm sat down the lake right now waiting for my wife to collect me. The tears are flowing and if anyone walks past now, they must think I'm crazy. I'm telling my story one bit at a time, Once I've told my story I may be finally able to let go. I'm sure there will be bumps in the road and some stumbles along the way, but I'm heading North.

The weird thing with trauma is… Sorry I can't remember, let me have a think….

Trauma Amnesia......

It's the brains way of protecting you, keeping you safe. Periods in time you just don't remember, Seconds, minutes, whole years of your life just not there anymore. My brains been working double shifts for the last thirty years, pretending this didn't exist. Pretending the heart attacks and the blood cancer doesn't matter, any crap I've had to deal with in my life doesn't matter. Stick it in the bottom of the filing cabinet, waiting to explode.

I wish I had said something at the time. I wish I had spoken up and shouted. I wish I had given my Martin Luther King speech.

I wish things were different but here we are.

We all have a story inside us. Some good, some bad. Sharing our stories, our memories that's how we write the story of our lives. We learn, we discover, we find out the worlds not such a bad place, that not everyone wants to hurt you. There are some amazing people out there and I'm hoping to be one of them people. Sharing my story with you so you can share yours. Maybe your loved one is reading this too, maybe it might give them an idea of what you're going through just remember, they are struggling too.

Trauma amnesia is where your brain just stops dead in its tracks. You could be talking about one thing then bang just stop and stare at the wall. You're lost for a few seconds, then back in the room. The lost memories that can haunt you in your sleep. I have this gift, well I'm not sure it's much of a gift. I can remember so much about my life and in great detail, the good and the bad. The things I have said and done. The places and people I have met along the way. The good ones that I wished I had stayed friends with. The bad ones that still live with me to this day.

I have memories in my head of me and him at his house. Lots of snap shots in the front room smoking and drinking, the things he used to do to me. Four other men have turned up. The tall ones got a plastic bag with cans of beer in it, they look like the cast of Auf-Wiedersehen Pet. I have images and flashbacks of us all sitting in his front room. Smoking and drinking having fun with me wearing some sort of sky-blue leather outfit, strapped up.

Then, of course, comes the good old Trauma Dump. I've given several out so far. You just spill your guts.

I was walking around the lake looking for birds to photograph with my camara. The beauty of summer, the trees all different shapes. The different shades of green, a kaleidoscope of colours in front of my eyes. Walking along the foot path staring at that little spot in the distance with my one eye, I feel like a cyclops. My eyes have joined together into one large one, it sits in the middle of my forehead. A man came up to me, I didn't see him at first as he was approaching outside of my peripheral vision.

"Hi. You, ok?"

I just looked at him and assessed him for the dangers. Although he was a small chap, It was clear he had a military career. I looked up

"Yeah, I'm ok".

We spent the next thirty minutes chatting. He got the lot, the grooming and the abuse, his friends. Everything. He also shared his own story with me. I don't know why I gave him a trauma dump. The only thing I can put it down to is this: even though we are able to talk to people, the pressure still builds up inside our heads. Trauma Dumping is a way of releasing that pressure before it explodes again. It's another way the brain is trying to protect you. Releasing all that energy brewing inside. Personally, I think anyone who is on the receiving end of a Trauma Dump they are a very privileged person. You don't plan to do a Trauma Dump. They just happen. This guy could see me walking along the footpath. He clearly knew what the thousand-yard stare was. Thank you, Martin, and, in fact, to both Martins and the other couple who helped me out just recently. That was the worst panic attack so far. They talked to me about my happy place.

"Can you talk to me about Santorini, please?"

Thank you SID.

I love spending time down at "The Dragonfly Café".

Trying to find the Otters. Looking for the Kingfishers.

The friendly Dragonflies all wanting to say "Hello"

I love nature it's great for your Mental Health.

Another of my happy places. My garden, I love sitting in the egg chair and watching the wildlife. Listening to the water and the birds singing. As always a good fire going to keep warm. I have no idea how I ended up living in such a beautiful house.

Chapter Thirteen
My Thoughts

My Happy Place. The sound of the stream in the distance.

*The birds singing away the Barn Owls and Red Kites
The jet-black star laden skies and a view over Pen Y Fan
Just me and the Wife, Scooby the dog and Iain bloody Stirling, the wife watches Love Island!
Gllfach Farm Holiday Accommodation. Sennybridge UK. I would quite happily live here for the rest of my life.*

People have always wanted to hurt me that's how I feel, either that or they let you down in some way. I haven't always been the friend I could have been to quite a few people. The trouble with me is this. With my strange belief that everyone wants to hurt me, the best thing to do is get in there first, either that or run away. That's how I have dealt with most things in my life. A constant life full of fight or flight. The more I can get out of the house and interact with the world, then the nicer people I hope to meet.

A good friend of mine keeps trying to get me out the house. I don't know how he puts up with me if I'm honest. He has just got into shooting, air rifle shooting, I loved shooting as a kid. He tries to get me up to the local gun club, it's an amazing place such a lovely location and loads of people use it. All day long all you can hear is shot guns going off, banging away. I haven't used a shot gun for years.

"Go on, go charge at him. Grab the gun off him. Turn the barrel around and put both barrels in your mouth. Pull the trigger."

I've nearly blown my head off before with a 12-bore twin barrel shotgun. God only knows how I didn't! I was pretty much staring down the barrel, looking at the swirly patterns, then BANG! I think it's best to avoid the gun club right now.

I have met some nice people from the fishing group I belong to. They have been offering me advice, where to fish and what baits to use. I've set myself a challenge this year, it's a way of trying to get me out the house, how to meet people and interact with the world. The challenge is to catch a 20lb plus carp, over 100lb of bream and 25lb plus of small roach and perch on the whip.

My wife likes me going fishing for two reasons. Firstly, it gets me out of the house, and secondly, the fishing kit I'm using used to belong to her dad. She loves to think a little part of him is with me when I'm on the bank. We have a lake within a few minutes' walk of our house. It's a great place to walk around and relax, and I'm always trying to encourage people to get out of the house. I'm passionate about Mental Health now. I've lived in silence for over thirty years, and it's nearly killed me several times over. Now, speaking out finally, it's the best thing I have ever done. Even though some days I wish I hadn't. Even though life is tough right now, even though I feel life is not worth living. I'm so glad that horrendous weight, so big and so draining, constantly pulling me back. I feel like I have been pulling a jumbo jet along a runway for most of my life. It's finally been released; my shoulders feel relaxed, and the stress and tension have lifted. Ok, it's been replaced for the time being with something equally horrendous, but I could never recover whilst I kept it a secret, kept it hidden. It would have always been there, growing and getting worse every second of the day. But do you know what, so what? Yes, I feel the same now, and some days worse, a lot worse. Trust me, I know. But at least now I can start to heal and finally talk about what happened. I can finally talk about how I'm feeling and maybe start to believe I can beat this. You can beat this; don't leave it like I did.

I was born with something called a pigeon chest. My ribs hadn't formed properly. It was touch and go as to whether I needed an operation as a baby to cut my rib cage open and fix me. It was a 50/50 chance of survival in them days. I feel I have come into this world in trauma, and that's no one's fault but him upstairs. I've endured trauma throughout my whole life, and it's getting worse. I don't know when level 10 and beyond will begin again or if it ever will. I constantly live with the worry that Level 10 is coming, and this time, I won't be able to stop it. I don't want my life to end with me still living in trauma. If you need to speak to someone, then please call the Samaritans.

You don't have to give your name or any details, and they won't try and track you. They will just listen to whatever you have to say. There will be no judgment no matter what's happened or how bad it was or may currently be. My counsellor, Cerian, used to work for the

Samaritans. They believe nobody should die alone. I didn't realise, but even in your darkest hour, when you need it the most. You hell bent on taking your own life, they can be there on the end of the phone. To be there for you when you take your last breath. All you have to do is dial 116 123. I don't think I want to die alone.

I'm passionate about Mental Health, and like most people who have gone through similar things, I have come up with an idea. It's an idea to help people who are suicidal or suffer from panic attacks. I call it SID. It stands for a Suicide ID. It's a credit card I had made. On one side, it has pictures of my family with some words that make sense to me. Reminders of what to do when I'm having a panic attack.

It has my name and the contact details of my wife printed on it. On the other side are more pictures of my happy place and some writing telling my family how much I love them and that I'm sorry for hurting them. I'm sorry I wasn't strong enough. Goodbye. When I'm feeling upset to the point I feel I can't carry on, I get the card out. I look at my wife on our wedding day with a beautiful smile on her face: Ladies Pavilion in Central Park, New York. I look at pictures of my children on our last holiday abroad, and they remind me of swimming with the sea turtles and spending happy times with mum and dad. I start the breathing technique that it reminds me to do. My mind can start to drift off to my happy place, Santorini, the sunsets over the distant horizon. I do all this because the card tells me to. I turn the card over and see me and my wife on top of a Welsh valley with Pen y Fan in the background. It's a beautiful summer's day, the rolling hills and the view for miles. The smile on my wife's face. I read the words that I want to say to my family, before I leave this world behind. So far, SID has a 100% success rate. It has had limited testing, but on them occasions, it's helped to have SID by my side. It doesn't matter what it is; have something on you that helps when you need it the most. Find a happy memory, a happy place you can take yourself to, even if it is Turf Moor!

"Happy place Turf Moor, Happy place Turf Moor"

I also have one of them Rubber Bracelets that I wear. I had some made for my campaign on SID. When I'm stressed, it's a comfort. I can flick it against my wrist or roll it around my palm. I've had them embossed and printed with the words.

"I'm in support of SID."

On the other side.

"I support Mental Health".

It's a catchy orange colour with green writing. I'm often running the band through my fingers. I can feel the bumps and the grooves as I'm spinning in over and over. It's quite relaxing. It's a grounding technique. When I find my mind going into a dark place, I have these things around me to help and calm me down.

I've been told that writing is good for you and even encouraged in terms of Mental Health. I'm not sure I've done the right thing by writing this, though. Most people write about their personal Mental Health problems and issues after they have received help and treatment. They have come through the other side, the Survivors. These people give me hope. These people give me inspiration to complete my day. Hope in the knowledge that one day I can be like them, I can call myself a survivor. At the moment, I need to concentrate on my recovery and getting better. That's why I need to be selfish and think of myself at the moment. My aim with this book is simple: don't hide what's happening or happened to you. People are there to talk to you in confidence if needed. It's not going to be easy but I hope I have prepared you for what may lie ahead. Even with all the knockbacks, the bad days, and the brick walls, I still believe this could be a world worth living in. Don't leave it too late like I did. It was the second biggest mistake of my life. The first was starting work at that care home. That place has ruined my life and I'm still letting it continue, and it needs to stop.

I find quotes quite helpful, especially the daily motivation quotes on social media as I'm Doom scrolling. They're not all good or interesting to me, however, but I'm going to share some with you. I believe they sum up what it feels like for me anyway. Here is one particular quote from Callum Hancock, another survivor who has offered me help and support. He is a true inspiration; you can read his story in the Sun newspaper. Callum said to me.

"When the clouds get heavy, it rains."

If you need to cry, then cry. Don't build it up. Let it out, let it go! Although I am totally aware that tears do dry up, and even when you need to cry, you just can't. Callum also told me how so many people reached out to him when he told his story. I believe even Roman Kemp can't go out of the house these days because people want to talk to him about their own Mental Health issues. I would love to be in a position to do that. Sadly, I need to take the time for me to get myself better. Feel free to visit my Instagram page. I hope it's going to be full of information, help, and tips for you and updates on my progress. When I can get around to sorting it out, this book is under a pseudonym. It's not because I don't care, and it's not because I want you to remain silent. It's the very opposite. It's me saying get help. My aim is to try to raise awareness of mental health, the good and the bad. To try to explain what it's really like, how it's not just a case of man up and get the fuck on with it. Sadly, it's real.

I'm going to get over this, I will get over this!

The trouble is I have so much information in my head, so much data to sort through, so many files. Getting them all in order and sifting through all that data morning, noon, and night.

I'm downloading it all from that Cloud, and I'm still on Dial-Up!

Some of the random things I come home with. Literary works of art, Shakespear to Mark Twain's Huckleberry Finn. Rex from Toy Story and Ancient Egyptian artifacts. I have quite a collection and love holding and talking about my pieces.

Chapter Fourteen
Jesus, he Knows Me

I wanted to touch on something that you might go through on this roller coaster journey you're on or thinking of taking. Just don't be scared.

Delusions

Originally, I used the Broadway-type set for that word simply because some of the things that I come up with and the thoughts that go through my head are worthy of an Oscar. I come up with some real wacky things at the moment. Just the other day, I was thinking Elon Musk was a Terminator sent back in time to destroy Mark Zuckerberg! Musk's plans are to stop Zuckerburg from creating the Metaverse, which will eventually turn into Skynet. Crazy right? Well, if you think that's mad you wait till you hear the latest. Currently, I think I might be Jesus 2.0! Before you think.

"What the hell is this kid smoking?"

Let me explain: me and the original baby Jesus 1.0 have quite a bit in common. I haven't seen anyone part the Red Sea, but I've swam in it. I'm a half-decent carpenter and have even seen swarms of locusts. I've walked over Brooklyn Bridge, so technically, I'm over water. I make homebrew, so I've literally turned water into wine. I have fed the crowds with fish at a charity event. Sadly, my Jason versus Goliath moments didn't work out for me, and worst of all, I've even met the Devil! Perhaps I should've titled this book the Bible 2.0.

What if Jesus was so traumatised in his early development? What if Jesus just could not stop thinking about his mum's possible affair? What if he developed a Personality Disorder? What if he was on shrooms for the first part of his life to try to deal with it all? Let's face it: he does look a bit like a hippy.

What if he just saw so much wacky stuff that he just had to write a book about it all? He just knew if he didn't, people would not believe him. That's what I would do.

I'm not Jesus 2.0. I do understand that. I know it's all in my head, but some days, it does make having a personality disorder fun and very interesting. Just remember you're not really an X-Man or Woman, or whatever the pronoun is nowadays. You're not a Scientist, Archaeologist, or Colt Seavers, so just manage your expectations, please. I have high expectations, and I don't think they are very realistic. I know I'm not going to be knighted by Prince William, then spend the evening watching England versus the All Blacks with Tindall and all the girls at Twickenham, all getting mortal. Just please, Kate, don't wear that green dress. I'm not going to get to speak to Prince Harry about his own Mental Health struggles and the old days around the Polo Field. It's quite sad as I've got a sibling I don't talk to. In reality, I would love to sit down with her in a room and talk. Just to listen to each other properly and resolve whatever has gone on in the past. You are my sister, after all, and I do love you.

Sadly, I don't think I'm going to get an honorary doctorate from Oxford, Cambridge, Yale, or Harvard. I don't think David Beckham is going to come around to my house for a BBQ and talk about his Mental Health. I'm not going to get together with Roman Kemp and introduce #SID to the world and help him with his Mental Health campaign. To be honest, this is the only part I hope does not come true. My wife's legs turn to jelly every time she sees his dad on TV. Sorry, Shirlie, but you may have a fight on your hands! I am not going to have the pleasure of attending my second-only football match at Turf Moor with Jordan North, and I don't think that every major sporting event will start with a minute silence to remember all those millions of people who have taken their own lives over the years. I'm not going to meet Elon Musk and ask him if the world is flat. Television networks aren't going to be queuing up and fighting over the rights to my story for the TV adaptation, I have some great ideas by the way, and sadly, I'm not going to spend a few days in a Thai jungle living off the land with Foxy and a film crew, discussing Mental Health for a TV series, trying to raise awareness. I'm probably not going to set up a charity organisation that visits schools where we can talk about internet safety and special friends, what to look out for, and how we can support friends with Mental Health issues.

I have a dream that there is going to be a huge global concert to raise awareness of Mental Health. Instead of Band-Aid, we can call it Bandage Aid, with all the proceeds going into Mental Health. We could all wear a badge in the shape of a blood-soaked bandage or a foam nose that looks like a bandage. I may be delusional and think I'm Jesus at the moment, but who doesn't think Band-Aid 2.0 would be an amazing idea, a global celebration and a day of music and fun, just like it was in 1985, all for Mental Health? However, it must contain a tribute to the late great Freddie Mercury. It would be amazing to release a charity single with Lady Gaga, but sadly, I don't think it's really going to happen. We are singing.

"Don't Give Up"

It's a Peter Gabrial and Jennifer Rush duet. To me, the words in that song are so powerful.

Rest your Head

You worry too much

It's going to be alright

When times get rough

You can fall back on us

Don't give up

Please don't give up

Thank you, Dad, for introducing me to it.

But what if!

I would build a huge building where people would come.

Cerian and I would give seminars talking about Mental Health. We would train the next generation of counsellors. That would be my Church, my Mosque, my temple of knowledge. Cerian will be one of my Apostles, helping me spread the word.

It's all just overthinking.

I might be Jesus 2.0; I might not be.

"I AM AN OVERTHINKER"

Shout it like I did. Delusions of grandeur are normal. They are not real, so just be mindful of them all. They can be quite funny, though, so just enjoy them for what they are and have a laugh about them. I'm sure Jesus wasn't on shrooms. He probably just received a good few WHACKS on the head as a kid, something I can relate to.

I have changed my mind, though, about Jesus and God or some sort of higher power. I guess something had to create us after all. Brian, honestly, mate, give me a ring. If a story like Jesus could possibly be true, the stories of a higher power might be, too. I'm going to keep an open mind and see what happens. I don't know what I'm going to be looking for, though. For all I know, it might be an elephant or a goat so I'm just going to try and be nice to everything and everyone from now on. It's a mad world out there. You never know that person standing next to you. The one with the big smile might be having a worse day than I am.

"I'm going to be kind today; I'm going to be the best version of myself I can be right now. I've got this

It wasn't my fault; I was a child, and you were an adult. I am not to blame. Turn the other cheek. My story has been bad and painful and cruel, but I am writing the next chapter, and it's not over."

I'm going to get that printed and read it every morning in front of a mirror until I start to believe it. I would love to see Cerian again and chat with her about what's been going on. We would have such a laugh about my beliefs. She gets me. Without her, there is no chance in this world I would be here today. She has had to sit and listen to my life events firsthand, in real-time, for the first time EVER!

I asked her once during one of our sessions if she believed me.

"Believe you, I could feel it!"

She deserves a knighthood, not me. It would be my privilege to join you at the event as I haven't seen William for years, and if I'm honest, the last time we met wasn't the happiest time of my life. I bet you laughed about me being a Royal Protection Officer. The reality was I was keeping an eye on all the little kids that played under that mighty Oak Tree, I knew where the Monsters Lair was, I knew where the Gargoyle was hiding, and not all bad people wear a vest with A.C.M.E. TNT strapped to it, and if watching Scooby Doo as a kid has taught me anything, it's that the real monsters are humans.

If you think Cerian deserves a medal, then God only knows what my wife deserves. You see, she is the one who holds me when I cry. She is the one who has to deal with my mood swings. The times when I have had a good week's fishing, she has seen me so happy. Then, the downs when my whole world collapsed, seriously falling apart to the point of death. She is my Princess Leia. I just wish I could give her more than what she deserves. I'm a bit of a burden to her and everyone right now, so thanks, Alwyn.

"MATE!"

One of the last things I want to talk about is something that not many people want to talk about, suicide!

Yes, at the moment, I feel suicidal, and it's not the nicest feeling in the world. Today has been a particularly tough day, and to be honest, I'm not sure why today is any different from yesterday or the day before. Today, things have just hit me, and in a big way. If I could take one single pill right now, and that pill made you go to sleep and never wake up, I would take it. It's not that I want to die. It's just I've had enough, and I don't want to do it anymore. I really worry that life is going to get too much, and I simply can't do it. Feeling so empty and feeling so down is all part of Mental Health, and it's where I am in my life right now. I haven't made any plans to kill myself, as that's not how my mind works. I just worry I'm going to say, that's it, I'm done, and something is going to happen that I don't have any control over. Suicidal feelings are not pleasant, and these are the times we need our loved ones around us. I've talked to my wife and told her how I'm feeling, and that's not an easy thing to do. No one wants to hear their loved one say.

"I've had enough, and I don't want to be here anymore."

Try not to beat yourself up for having suicidal thoughts, as you're probably going to get this feeling at some point. Just remember to talk to someone about how you're feeling and seek help if required. I believe in you.

SID-Suicide ID

When I'm having a bad time and need help, I can look at my SID card and think of happier times. Holidays with the Family and a picture of my wife on our Wedding Day. It has emergency contact details and information that helps me, including notes about my happy place. The reverse is a view from the little Shepards Hut overlooking Pen Y Fan with some words I want to say to my family before I leave this world. When I feel suicidal, these things calm me down and keep me grounded. My rubber bracelet that I can run through my fingers. I even have a keyring #SID.

It's because of the Kelly Foundation that I find myself in front of a new Mental Health Nurse called Kat, and we all need a Kat in our lives. I honestly feel I have someone in the NHS fighting in my corner for the very first time. Thank you so much. Kat gave me a copy of the referral form that was sent to the Mental Health Team. The reports are hard for me to read, albeit not quite accurate. I'm not single, and half of my medical history is missing.

NHS
Avon and Wiltshire Mental Health Partnership
NHS Trust

PCLS (TRIAGE) REFERRAL FORM

PLEASE NOTE: NO FAX REFERRALS WILL BE ACCEPTED BY THE PCLS (TRIAGE) SERVICE
Email to awp.swindonpclsreferrals@nhs.net

Urgency of assessment

Please indicate the urgency of this referral, i.e. how quickly do you feel that the patient needs contact from the service.

This is based on your clinical judgement and risk assessment. However, following triage by a Mental Health professional the timeframe to assessment may be amended in line with the UK Triage Scale. You will be notified of referral outcome by letter or email, following triage.

We will attempt to make contact within 72 hours unless the assessment is urgent. Please ensure that the patient's contact details are up to date and please make them aware that we will call from a withheld number.

Emergency/4 hour referrals

For emergency/4 hour referrals, please contact your local PCLS service using the numbers below.

BSW	BNSSG
Bath —	North —
Swindon —	South Gloucestershire —
Wiltshire —	

Urgent/routine referrals:

☐ Within 72 hours	x Within 4 weeks
Urgent mental health response	Routine mental health response
Please complete and submit this referral form to PCLS and then contact your local PCLS service using the numbers above.	Please complete and submit this referral form to PCLS.

Is this patient known to AWP services or was discharged from services within the last 3 months?
x Yes ☐ No

Patient details (details pulled directly from your clinical system)		Referrer details	
Full Name:		Date of referral:	09 Aug 2023
	Preferred name:		
Gender:	Male	Referring GP:	Kathryn Finch
	D.O.B:		
NHS No:		Registered GP name & address:	
	Marital status:	Single person	
Address:	Postcode:	Referring GP	

Reason for referral – Referrals may be rejected without this information

Please provide a narrative of your concerns about this patient's mental state to include why he/she requires secondary mental health services and what you require from our assessment. Please also indicate what interventions you have tried in primary care prior to making this referral e.g. talking therapies, social prescribing, medication:

E: ▇▇▇▇ reports that he is up and down, no change from last time he spoke to anyone.
PCLS referral reported to have been completed by therapist. He spoke to someone from PCLS a few months ago and was told he does not have a PD - this was based on a 10 minute phone call.
Had 6 months counselling with IPSUM, seeing a psychotherapist through Kelly Foundation.
▇▇▇▇ unsure if he has a disassociative disorder or bipolar so is asking for psychoanalysis ▇▇▇▇ his is that he cannot receive appropriate therapy until he has been assessed.

▇▇▇▇ expectation is that the NHS comes up with an action plan to provide support and appropriate care pathway – PD assessment suggested.

Struggling in the world - cannot go outside due to anxiety and paranoia that people want to kill him, and that he may bump into an abuser without knowing that is who they are.
Logic is everything.
Often regresses into childhood state.
Feels he has several alter ego's.
Sees the world in black and white - feels very let down by people when they say they will do something and don't.
Struggles to form and maintain relationships.
Cannot work as he is unable to have faith in relationships he builds at work, this is as he has been abused in one way or another in all jobs he has had.
Substance misuse - spent 30 years being a functioning alcoholic, dabbling in drugs and had a strong gambling addiction. Now drinks weekly with his wife.
Police involvement - no criminal record. Small amount of undetected petty crimes committed - none serious.
Self harm - past substance misuse, poor dietary intake intensively. On chemotherapy pills for blood cancer (body produces blood clots) but does not take these as he feels he may then get a large blood clot and die in his sleep.
Self neglecting - showers weekly if that, will put on whatever clothes he finds on the floor.
Suicide attempts - does not want to be here any day, at all. Constant strong suicidal ideation. No intent expressed but feels certain "the switch will flip". In his words he lives constantly between 7-9 on scale of 1-10 of suicidality.
Struggles with maintaining a job.
Constant flashbacks of what happened to him, smells, sensing being touched and hearing his abusers voice.
Always has an exit plan for everywhere he goes.

Childhood - significant childhood sexual trauma. No domestic abuse recalled. Constant bullying in school, no friends throughout this time. Dad was in the army so had a transient life. Left school at 16, met a friend in an old people's home who was older and groomed him followed by introducing him to others to abuse and rape him. Cannot recall how many times he has been raped and by who. P. Refer to PCLS for assessment of PD.

Risk to self and others

Please ensure you answer all of the following for the safety of patient, staff and the public.

	Yes	No	Not Known
1. Is this person expressing thoughts of suicide or self-harm?	x	☐	☐
If the answer to the above question was yes, please provide details **Constantly**			
2. Has the person ever made a suicide or self-harm attempt?	x	☐	☐
If the answer to the above question was yes, please provide details			
3. Is the person expressing thoughts or has previously engaged in episodes of violence/aggression?	x	☐	☐
If the answer to the above question was yes, please provide details			

4. Is the home environment safe to visit?	X	☐	☐
If the answer to the above question was yes, please provide details			
5. Is there concern about harm or exploitation from others e.g. domestic violence, sexual harassment or abuse, financial abuse?	☐	☐	☐
If the answer to the above question was yes, please provide details **No concern from referrer, serious concern from Michael**			
6. Are there any child protection/safeguarding issues?	☐	X	☐
If the answer to the above question was yes, please provide details			
7. Does the patient have any dependents/children/vulnerable adults/pets?	☐	X	☐
If the answer to the above question was yes, please provide details			
8. Is the person at risk of self-neglect, physically or emotionally?	X	☐	☐
If the answer to the above question was yes, please provide details **Self neglect**			
9. Is there concern about the person's general current behaviour e.g. risk taking, sleep pattern, activities of daily living?	X	☐	☐
If the answer to the above question was yes, please provide details **Sleep, mood, ADL's**			
10. Is there a history of misusing drugs or alcohol?	X	☐	☐
If the answer to the above question was yes, please provide details **30 years of substance misuse**			
11. Is there a history of depression or serious mental illness, including any current episode?	☐	☐	X
If the answer to the above question was yes, please provide details			
12. Does the person have a shotgun/firearm licence?	☐	X	☐
If the answer to the above question was yes, please provide details			

Patient Consultations [Please upload latest results directly from GP system]
Please provide last few consultations, wherever possible

Patient Problems [Please upload latest results directly from GP system]

Depression - motion (X76x6): Aug 1998
Suicide risk, no (Y08Ae): Sep 1998
Depression resolved (XaLC0): Jul 2008
Acute non-ST segment elevation myocardial infarction (XaleY): Jun 2010
Insertion of coronary artery stent (X00IJ): Jun 2010
Ischaemic heart disease (XE2uV): Jun 2010
Percutaneous balloon angioplasty of coronary artery (7928.): Jun 2010

Anxiety disorder (E200.), Jul 2010
Exercise tol/er test equivocal (33B94), Aug 2010
Anxiety state NOS (E200z), Sep 2010
Coronary arteriograph. abnormal (5543.), Nov 2010
Coronary artery bypass grafting (X00tE), Jan 2011
Deep vein thrombosis of lower limb (Xa9Bs), Aug 2018
Echocardiography (X77c1), Aug 2018
Prostatic hyperplasia unspecified (K200.), Aug 2018
Essential thrombocythaemia (X20FX), Nov 2018
Post-traumatic stress disorder (X00Sf), Aug 2022
Panic disorder (XE1Y7), Aug 2022
Enhanced review indicated before granting access to own health record (Y2ffe), Oct 2022
Ischaemic heart disease, 2009
Acute non-ST segment elevation myocardial infarction, Jun 2010
Anxiety disorder, Jul 2010
Deep vein thrombosis of lower limb, Aug 2018
Pulmonary embolus, Aug 2018
Echocardiography, Aug 2018
Prostatic hyperplasia unspecified, Aug 2018
Essential thrombocythaemia, Nov 2018
Myeloproliferative disorder, Feb 2019
Venesection, Jun 2022
Post-traumatic stress disorder, Aug 2022
Enhanced review indicated before granting access to own health record, Oct 2022

Current medication being prescribed at date of referral [Please upload latest results directly from GP system]

Acutes — Hydroxycarbamide 500mg capsules. Supplied by GWH haematology
Repeats — Ramipril 2.5mg capsules, ONE capsule to be taken ONCE a day, to reduce blood pressure, help kidneys and reduce risk of heart attack or stroke
Rivaroxaban 20mg tablets, ONE tablet to be taken ONCE a day WITH FOOD to thin the blood and help prevent strokes as directed. lifelong
Sertraline 100mg tablets. Take TWO tablets daily
Omeprazole 20mg gastro-resistant capsules, take one daily
Atorvastatin 20mg tablets, ONE tablet to be taken DAILY to lower cholesterol levels
Bisoprolol 2.5mg tablets. ONE tablet to be taken ONCE a day
Glyceryl trinitrate 400micrograms/dose pump sublingual spray, Use ONE to TWO sprays under the tongue when required for the relief of chest pain

Confirmed allergies at date of referral [Please upload latest results directly from GP system]

SIMVASTATIN
No known allergies

Recent diagnostics [Please upload latest results directly from GP system]

Alcohol Consumption:
Smoking: Ex-smoker
Illicit substances:

Chapter Fifteen
The Quotes

EXCLUSIVE

News > UK News

POLO CLUB PAEDO Polo club worker was abused by paedophile bar boss while Prince Charles drank next door

Victim said he wanted to tell the royals about the abuse he endured at the hands of a paedophile club boss

Ben Griffiths
Published: 22:30, 4 Aug 2018 | Updated: 22:41, 4 Aug 2018

It was this story.

I knew I would be believed now.

I would love to speak to the person behind this and the other "Boys" that he borrowed. It was this story that broke my silence for the very first time, and for that, I'm truly thankful to you. My biggest fear is that you were the "Boy" behind me. Maybe that should be the next book.

"Call of the Void"

Volume II

"The Boy who came after"

I'm so sorry I was weak and I could not protect you. I'm so sorry I failed you and you had to suffer. I don't know if I can ever forgive myself for that.

With myself and my mental illness it's similar to many others. We won't tell you what's really happening inside us. When you ask if I'm okay, sure, yeah, I'm okay. That's the answer you're going to get.

"I'm Okay."

The real answer is.

"I'm br***OK***en."

I have seen a campaign started by Roman Kemp; it's about asking the question twice. Sometimes, the second response can be different from the first. Please ask your friends if they are OK. When they say "I'm OK," ask them again.

"Are you really okay?"

It's a fact that too many men hide their feelings and their thoughts. We hide behind masculinity. It's time to start challenging and questioning these thoughts. It's time for us men to start talking before it gets too late.

When people message me and ask how I'm doing, this is how the conversations go.

"Hi mate. How are things going. You, okay?"

"Yeah, **I'M** good, thanks, mate. **SORRY** not been around much. So much going on with appointments and all. **I**'m **FEEL**ing Good at the moment. Don't get me wrong, it's a challenge some days. You have to learn to adapt and take each day as it comes; otherwise, it will eat you up and kill you, and I don't **LIKE** the sound of that. **I** don't **WANT TO DIE** well, not just yet. Thank you for the message, and let's meet up soon. Might not be able to do it next week, so maybe the week after. *I* need to sort stuff out at the doctor's. More changes to my medication. Keep taking the pills. At least, it stops me **FEEL**ing **SUICIDAL** pmsl. I will give you a shout in the middle of next week. Take care and say hi to the Mrs".

We hide ourselves away from others. We don't want to worry them; you start to distance yourself from family and friends.

"Isolation comes because you don't want to be a burden to others. They don't understand" *Unknown Author.*

What people struggle to realise is. What this is doing inside your whole body, Inside your head.

"You can be doing okay but all it takes is one trigger and your world comes crashing down." *Unknown Author.*

This is so true I'm aware of so many triggers it's unreal. I have learned about my window of tolerance, how I'm feeling and when I need to take action, when I need to talk and not bottle it up. Someday

I'm at level 4 then something will come on the TV or in the Newspapers, maybe just something you overhear. The feelings and flashbacks hit you like a freight train. It's like you're back at the beginning where it all started.

"What do you fancy for dinner tonight? Shall we do a roast for dinner?"

"Are we having chicken?"

Going over and reliving what happened. Tolerance right up to level nine. I don't like level ten. That's when SID comes out. Even though you're going through a lot right now, don't beat yourself up. Listen to what your body is telling you.

"Sometimes self-care is not always going to appointments and taking your medication. Sometimes, self-care is just getting out of bed. Having breakfast then going back to bed. Someday, it means you have to cry all day. Sometimes it involves doing nothing at all." *Unknown Author.*

"Please do not mistake a bad day for being weak. It's not weakness. The bad days that's when you're trying your hardest". *Unknown Author*

"It may not look like you haven't done much today, but mentally, it's been a very busy day, and it's left me exhausted." *Unknown Author.*

Them days you can spend in bed, nothing willing you to get up. My wife is very supportive and is very understanding. She realises what sort of mood I'm in. She knows when I need a cuddle or a shoulder to cry on, someone to talk to. Her to be there and talk to about anything, no matter how bad. I understand it's hard for her to see me like this. She so badly wants to take it all away.

"The trouble with Mental Health is you can slip from being perfectly fine one minute then falling apart the next." *Unknown Author.*

When people say things to me like

"You need to start getting over this."

The answer I so want to give is

"Why can't you accept that these things are happening to me? Why can't you see the damage this has done to me? How deep the damage really is?" *Unknown Author.*

Having Anxiety, Depression, or PTSD, any Mental Illness. It's a silent and very painful experience. It makes little to no sense. You just sit there and suffer alone, alone in deadly silence.

"I still have a long way to go, but I'm already so far from where I used to be. I'm proud of that" *Unknown Author.*

"Be gentle with yourself. You're doing the best you can right now, and that is always enough." *Unknown Author.*

I use these ones quite a lot. I just wish people could see the real me. Understand what I'm trying to tell you.

It just feels a little difficult to actually tell you the truth.

"I'm fine"	– I'm not fine, please help me.
"I'm just tired"	– I can't take any more of this.
"I already ate"	– I can't be bothered to eat.
"It's fine, you can go"	– Please don't leave me.
"I'm ok"	– I'm completely broken and want to die..
"I slept well"	– I had a rubbish sleep, only 4 hours.

I haven't given you a list here, so you can start making excuses. I'm trying to let your loved ones know what to look out for. When you could do with a hug or a chat. I cry a lot most days. Crying gets hard. Believe it or not, I keep running out of tears. The times the clouds get so heavy, I just want to release the rain, but the rain doesn't come, just more thunder and lightning. When I do cry, I still try to hide it, and I have no idea why. When my wife catches me crying in secret, that's when we talk. That's when I can release the pain inside me.

It's such an easy thing to do, hiding your tears. The fake yawn is always a classic. Wearing sunglasses around the house, desperately trying to hide the tears falling down your face, rolling down your cheeks. Summer is great, hay fever season. Yes, you can develop it at any time.

Look out for eating, too. A well-balanced diet is good for your Mental Health. I keep trying to tell myself that. Today's meals have consisted of three ice pops, some mint imperials, and a packet of crab sticks.

Don't lie to your loved ones. They are helping you.

"Have you eaten today?"

"Not yet, but I'm not that hungry. I will have something later."

"Go downstairs now and have something to eat, please."

"I will. I'm going okay".

Walking into the kitchen, grabbing a bowl from the cupboard. Placed it down on the side, proceeded to open the fridge, unscrewed the milk lid, and started to pour. Not too much milk, just enough to make it look like the bowl has been used. Before loading it into the dishwasher, don't forget the spoon.

Please don't end up like me. I'm a bitter and twisted individual with serious Mental Health problems, not to mention cancer and a heart condition. I'm a walking stroke just waiting to happen. Make your

"I Have a Dream Speech"

Shout it from the rooftops if you need to. Just don't hide in silence.

You have already suffered the worst. You got this. Don't let it kill you because it will try. Believe me, it will try.

My beautiful lake as dawn breaks, My quest to catch a 20lb Carp!

It's not going that well!!

I started fishing here as a junior over 30 years ago. It holds a special place for me now.

I AM NOT DAMAGED GOODS
I AM GOLD REFINED
IN A CRUCIBLE
Carolyn Spring

Kintsugi has helped me understand there is Hope.

I can rebuild, to become better and stronger.

It's an Ancient Japanese art form.

They break a bowl or a cup, something made from China.

I did one from a Teacup.

Gave it a few knocks with a hammer till it broke up a little.

Then glued it back together with a paint I made.

A Beautiful Gold Paint.

Yes, you could see all the cracks, but them cracks had healed. Them cracks were part of a past event that no longer exists.

Them cracks are now healing, making you a more beautiful person.

Because even when something is broken. It can be fixed. Mended in a more beautiful way.

IM NOT MAD IM NOT CRAZY
IM JUST TRAUMATISED
Carolyn Spring

I totally get this, although I do think I'm a little crazy!

I SURVIVED THE WORST, AS A CHILD, ON MY OWN

SO, I CAN SURELY SURVIVE THIS

NOW AS AN ADULT, WITH SUPPORT

I AM RESILIENT AND I AM STRONG

BECAUSE I HAVE ALREADY SURVIVED THE WORST

I GOT THIS

Carolyn Spring

www.carolynspring.com

I guess she has a point.

Nobody really knows how much anyone else is hurting. We could be standing next to someone who is completely broken and we'd never know. So please be kind always.

"To anyone who is struggling and doesn't think they can live like this much longer. Remember you have survived 100% of your bad days so far".

Unknown Author

My friend Callum said this to me at the very start.

"It's like a roller coaster journey so buckle up and enjoy the ride."

That reminded me of a song I liked from back in the day.

"She said hello you fool I love you. Come on join the joy ride. Be a joyrider"

"Get your tickets here. Step right this way."

Second verse same as the first.

Sorry, it's not quite the end. Don't forget I overthink everything. I do feel like I have a right to be a victim at the moment because that's exactly what I am. I am a victim of sexual abuse; there, I've said it. I'm just trying to turn from being a victim into something else. My intentions were always to take this to the grave, but I just couldn't the stress and anxiety all these years. The countless songs that I listen to over and over again in my head, constantly singing the same lines.

"Keep running up that hill."

I'm glad to see times are changing. I'm glad to see men are starting to talk more about their Mental Health, even if the NHS is playing catch up. We are in the grasp of an unseen Global Pandemic, and it's getting worse. I also have to say I'm glad to see programmes like Eastenders doing storylines on Mental Health. Just be warned, it's not all like you see on TV. They have been very good, except for a few small things, and they are big things. You don't just get an assessment overnight; you don't just get into counselling within a week because you can pay for it. You probably won't get bumped up the list because of a cancellation. Mental Health takes some time to get over. In reality, you never will. It will always be a part of your life. We just have to find a way to deal with it. These things take time, and sadly, if you have little or no money, the wait is even longer. I'm Glad the world is trying to change to be a better place, even if we do have a way to go. When we were kids, we used the "N" word every time we played hide and seek. We didn't know any better; that's just how things were. Times are changing, and it's a great thing to see. I do believe together, we can make a difference. We can help and support those around us, and if you're listening up there.

"Dear God. I'm still waiting for that Lottery win. Can you make it this weekend, please? It's a rollover. Thank you"

For me, writing my story has really helped me to understand what, how, and why these things happened to me. I would encourage anyone with a story to write their own book.

I would love a whole series of books called "Call of the Void" to be published not only for your own personal Mental Health but to raise awareness of these things. The more we can get the message out, the more people may understand, and hopefully, the more people we can ultimately save.

"Call of the Void"

Volume III

"The Gospel according to Josh"

I thought Josh was a complete knob when I first met him, but to be fair, he thought the same about me, but then I got to know him. Josh, or as I call him, Noah stepped up when a Disaster struck. He saved many, many creatures from a horrid death. The story was in the national newspapers, and Noah made the national news. Josh is a top bloke, believe it or not, and also an amazing Carp Angler. His dream is to be sponsored by Nash Fishing Tackle, and in my opinion, they should snap him up. I would love to write Call of the Void Volume III one day; Josh has had a crazier life than mine! Here, he is holding a beautiful fish from my local lake. Josh fishes for his own personal Mental Health, and you can see what it means to him when he catches a fish of such beauty. The look on his face to me simply says, "Thank you, this one's for you, Dumbo." Thank you for everything you have done for the Angling Club, Noah, stay safe, bro.

Take care all, just be mindful of that old saying.

"Life has a way of messing you up sometimes. Giving you a kick when your down."

Asda have moved all their shelves around and that challenge I set myself to catch all them fish from my local lake.

It's over; all the fish have died!

If you wish to show your support, please visit
Peatmoor Angling Go-FundMe

About 20 people a day commit Suicide in the UK.

Worldwide, it's about 2,000. Nearly Three Quarters of a Million People Every Year. Out there in the world right now, there is someone who has had enough. This minute someone has felt they could no longer be here and doesn't want to be part of this world anymore. Every minute, in truth, about every 45 seconds of every day, another statistic in the making. The dial on the Worldwide Suicide Counter, ticking over one more digit. Repeat the process every 45 seconds. The trouble is the counter is getting faster, speeding up. I wonder where the acceptable number lies. Another one before you even finished this paragraph.

As of today, Saturday 2nd December 2023, 16:55 GMT

986,166 people have committed suicide this year alone.

Today, the figure stands at 2,071, So far.

So many pointless deaths. So many wasted lives, so little help!

I want to dedicate this

book to millions of people I really do, but there are two people that have come into my life. Two people who I feel I owe everything to.

First and foremost is my wife. Thank you for being the one. The one who has to deal with me. Thank you for keeping me grounded. Thank you for being you. I seriously love you.

The next person is Cerian Lye-Owens. She found the strength to deal with me, and I could see how tough it was sometimes. Thank you for everything you have ever done for me. You are a truly inspirational person, and I thank you from the bottom of my heart for everything you did for me. I will never forget you.

This book is also dedicated to all those who have lost the struggle. Please

"Don't Give Up"

Thank you for taking the time to read my book and hear my story. I hope you have gained an insight on how Mental Health can affect people, how these horrendous things can happen? How we deal with them and ultimately how we try and recover. I wish you all good luck and a life full of peace and happiness. Thank you. Please take care of yourself and your loved ones.

Please don't forget to ask the question.

"Are you Ok?"

"No really, are you OK?"

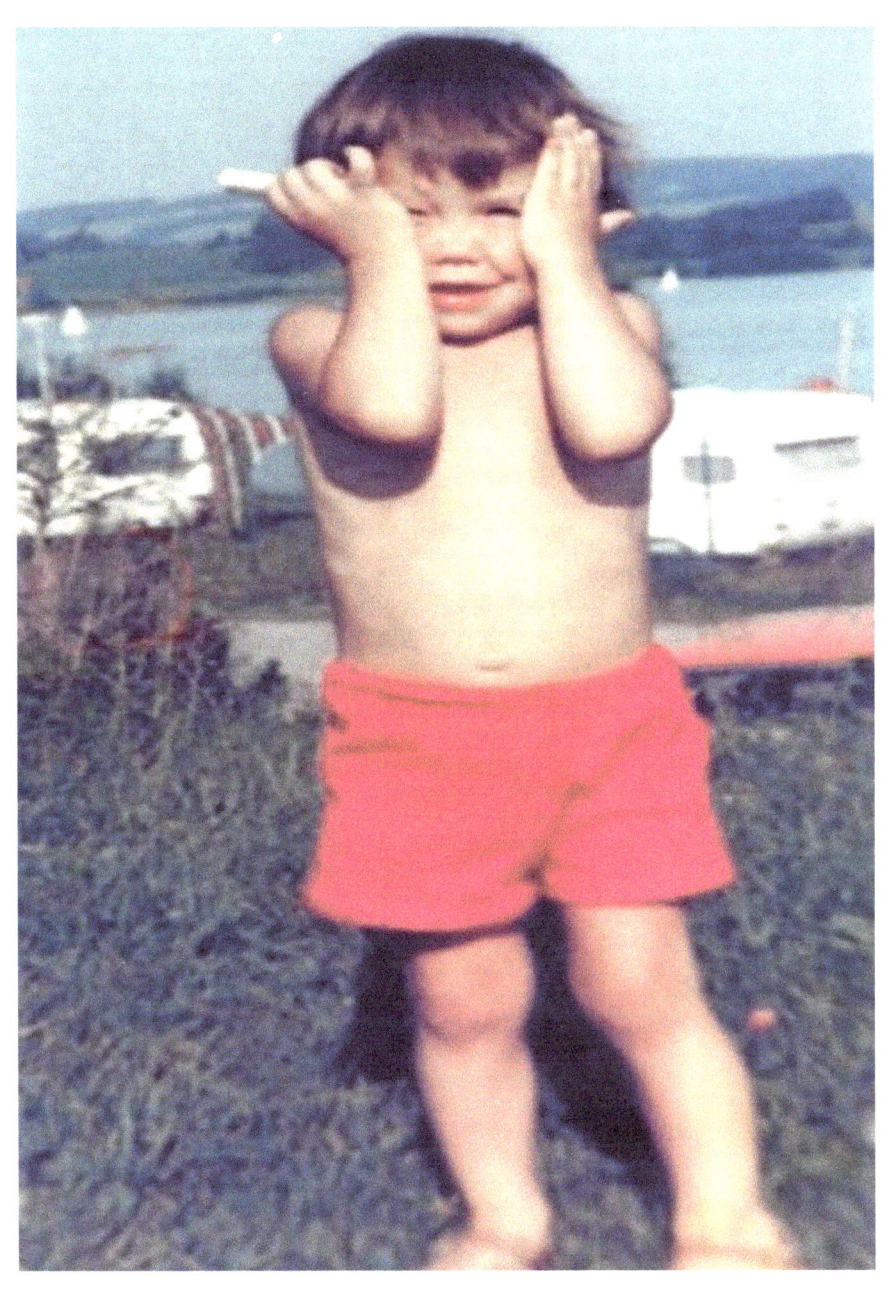

To be Continued……..

If you have enjoyed reading Volume I, then please keep an eye out for future Volumes, hopefully in the planning.

Call if the Void

Volume II

"The boy who came after"

It's the story of the boy who broke his silence. The boy who made me stand up. The boy who made me think I could be believed. It's how this happened to him. The police operation to catch our abuser and put him behind bars. It's a story of how the boy who came after dealt with it all and how he now lives his own life.

Call of the Void

Chapter III

"The gospel, according to Josh"

The story about Josh, aka Noah. How he ended up in a police cell, how he was abused. How he hid under the tables at school and wouldn't come out. How ADHD and naughty kid syndrome works! How we bonded over our stories together on our lake, all about our dogs and blue cheese. How fishing and nature are helping us heal. How we talk about abuse!

Call of the Void

Volume IV

"And in the Blue corner"

How does a Roughneck Championship boxer get abused? The story of what happened and how it all happened. Callum's ups and his downs. How do you survive!

Milton Keynes UK
Ingram Content Group UK Ltd.
UKHW050300080124
435633UK00001B/2